growth psychology

models of the healthy personality

Duane Schultz
The American University

D. VAN NOSTRAND COMPANY
New York   Cincinnati   Toronto   London   Melbourne

D. Van Nostrand Company Regional Offices:
New York   Cincinnati

D. Van Nostrand Company International Offices:
London   Toronto   Melbourne

Copyright © 1977 by Litton Educational Publishing, Inc.

Library of Congress Catalog Card Number: 76–47206
ISBN: 0–442–27434–3

Published by D. Van Nostrand Company
450 West 33rd Street, New York, N.Y. 10001

10 9 8 7 6 5 4 3 2

preface

A radical change is occurring in the way in which some psychologists are viewing the human personality. The new focus and direction is called "growth psychology" or "health psychology," and it is concerned not with the sick side of human nature (psychological illness) but with the healthy side (psychological "wellness"). The purpose of growth psychology is not to treat victims of neuroses and psychoses, but to tap and release the vast human potential for actualizing and fulfilling one's capabilities and for finding a deeper meaning in life. In short, growth psychology attempts to expand, enlarge, and enrich the human personality, quite a change from the previous emphasis.

People of all ages, in all walks of life, are enthusiastically embracing the human potential movement. Sensitivity sessions, T-groups, and other forms of encounter therapy are immensely popular as more and more Americans become concerned with actualizing, fulfilling, and expanding their selves in order to reach heightened levels of awareness. A variety of schemes and prescriptions for achieving self-actualization is offered in semiprofessional and popular books and in magazine articles. With almost messianic fervor, practitioners and followers of the human potential movement explore their own inner natures and, apparently (although the evidence is far from complete), are finding the sense of identity, autonomy, and fulfillment that the older, traditional approaches to psychology fail to provide (or even to recognize).

Interest in growth psychology is nowhere stronger than in the college classroom; many students have come to look upon this new area as an instrument of personal and social salvation. College courses on the healthy personality are being offered, and traditional courses in personality and adjustment are shifting their emphasis from the study of the sick to the study of the well.

This book focuses on one major aspect of the study of the healthy personality: the theoretical rationales or models that attempt to define the nature of this enriched human life. Written at a level that presupposes little formal training in psychology, the book is intended as a supplementary text for courses in personal adjustment and those dealing exclusively with the healthy personality. Seven models of the healthy personality are discussed: those of Gordon Allport, Carl Rogers, Erich Fromm, Abraham Maslow, Carl Jung, Viktor Frankl, and Fritz Perls.

Not all of these theorists are identified explicitly with the human potential movement, but they all address themselves to the same problem: What is the nature of the healthy personality? Each theorist offers his own unique view of and prescription for psychological growth and fulfillment. They each see, from different perspectives, the potential in us to be better or more than we are, and they each present their own definition of the heights of full humanness to which we should aspire. They each believe that psychological health is a good deal more than merely an absence of neurosis or psychosis.

With each theorist I have tried to show how certain experiences in his personal life have influenced his work and his view of human nature. In some cases this relationship is more direct and obvious than in others. As we shall see, some of the theories are mirror images of the men who proposed them. In all cases, the theories are expressions of dynamic insights on the part of their originators as well as profound observations and interpretations of the theorists' views of what it means to be a human being. They each have something unique and important to say to us.

The theories are not discussed in any order of importance; those at the end of the book are no less worthwhile than those that begin it. I have presented each theory as objectively as possible, trying to keep my own personal and professional biases out of the discussion. I save my own view for the end of each chapter where, under the title "A Personal Comment," I discuss my own reaction to each view. Please bear in mind when you read those sections that my reaction is personal. I am not speaking for psychology or for anything or anyone other than myself. These are comments that I hope will lead to critical speculation and inquiry by you, the reader. They are intended to provoke, not to indoctrinate. In a sense, they are my indulgence and reward for writing the book.

I am grateful to my wife, Sydney Ellen, for her professional and personal support. In the midst of her graduate studies, she somehow found time to research the literature, edit the manuscript, and make valuable suggestions on matters of style and content.

Duane Schultz

contents

1

The healthy personality

What is a healthy personality? What are the characteristics of the person who has a healthy personality? How does this person behave and think and feel? Can you or I become healthy personalities?

These questions are being asked with increasing frequency not only by psychologists but by millions of others as well. Predictably, not far behind these questions there has appeared a variety of answers—a surge of self-help books, guiding credos, promises of new life styles—some over-simplified and glib (and worthless), and others of potential value in helping us to better understand ourselves.

Large numbers of Americans are groping in groups, exploring and exposing their inner selves (and bodies) in sensitivity sessions, T-groups, and a host of other forms of encounter therapy. Criminals and drug addicts, students and teachers, workers and executives, young and old, fat and thin are apparently finding in such experiences dimensions and potentials in their personalities that they never realized they possessed.

The theme of this highly popular movement is to find and define a healthier personality. The emphasis is not so much on healing childhood-related conflicts and past emotional wounds as on releasing hidden reservoirs of talent, creativity, energy, and motivation. The focus is toward what a person can become, not what he or she has been or is at the moment.

The study of the human potential for growth was ignored for a long time in psychology, which examined primarily mental illness, not mental health. In recent years, however, a growing number of psychologists are coming to recognize the capacity for growth and change in the human personality.

These "growth psychologists" (most of them consider themselves to be humanistic psychologists) have taken a fresh look at human nature. What they see is a different kind of person from that depicted by behaviorism and psychoanalysis, the traditional forms of psychology.

Humanistic psychologists have been critical of these traditions because they believe that behaviorism and psychoanalysis offer limited views of human nature, ignoring the heights to which persons have the potential to rise. Behaviorism, these critics charge, treats the human being as a machine—"a complex system behaving in lawful ways."[1] The individual is depicted as a well-ordered, regulated, predetermined organism with as much spontaneity, vivacity, and creativity as a thermostat. Psychoanalysis has given us only the sick or crippled side of human nature because it focuses on neurotic and psychotic behavior. Freud, and those who followed his teachings, studied the emotionally disturbed, not the healthy, personality—the worst of human nature, not the best.

Neither behaviorism nor psychoanalysis has dealt with our potential for growth, our desire to be better or more than we are. Indeed, these viewpoints offer a pessimistic picture of human nature. We are seen by behaviorists as passive responders to external stimuli and by psychoanalysts as victims of biological forces and childhood conflicts.

To the growth psychologists, human beings are much more than that. While most growth psychologists do not deny that external stimuli, instincts, and childhood conflicts influence personality, they do not believe that human beings are unchangeable victims of these forces. We can and must rise above our past, our biological nature, and the features of our environment. We must develop and grow beyond these potentially inhibiting forces. The growth psychologist's image of human nature is optimistic and hopeful. They believe in our capacity for expanding, enriching, developing, and fulfilling ourselves, to become all we are capable of becoming.

Supporters of the human potential movement suggest that there is a desirable level of growth and development that goes beyond "normality," and they argue that it is necessary for human beings to strive for that advanced level of growth in order to realize, or *actualize,* all of their potential. In other words, it isn't enough just to be free of emotional illness; the absence of neurotic or psychotic behavior is not sufficient to qualify one as a healthy personality. The absence of emotional illness is no more than a necessary first step to growth and fulfillment. The individual must reach further.

1. B. F. Skinner, *Beyond Freedom and Dignity* (New York: Knopf, 1971), p. 202.

This position may disappoint those who feel that they have enough difficulty just trying to stay free of mental illness. Now they are told that being normal is not good enough, that they are missing out on some higher level of human growth, some "supernormality." But what is wrong with being simply normal? Isn't it possible to have a rich, meaningful life (as long as one is free of neuroses or psychoses) without having to move on to a higher level of development? You may already know the answers to these questions from your own experience. It is possible to be entirely normal (in the sense of having no emotional illness and of having your needs and drives well satisfied) and yet be miserable at the same time.

If we believe the growth psychologists (and perhaps our own experience), we agree that it is possible to have all facets of life functioning satisfactorily and still suffer agonizing boredom, stagnation, hopelessness, and meaninglessness. Even in the face of seemingly ideal conditions, we may feel a yawning void in our lives, as though something essential were missing, yet we cannot identify what's wrong. We may live comfortably, have a secure job and a warm and loving family, be free of worry, and yet not know any great joy, any overwhelming enthusiasm, any intense feeling of dedication or commitment. Obviously, all is not well—our lives are not as complete as they could be, in spite of the surface appearance.

The Russian novelist Leo Tolstoy wrote a haunting description of a man for whom, on the surface, everything was ideal. Yet the man was gripped by such an overwhelming sense of meaninglessness that he trembled on the edge of suicide. "Why should I live?" he asked. Tolstoy knew well the pain he was describing, for he was writing about himself.

> I felt that something had broken within me on which my life had always rested, that I had nothing left to hold on to, and that morally my life had stopped. . . .
> Behold me then, a man happy and in good health, hiding the rope in order not to hang myself to the rafters of the room where every night I went to sleep alone; behold me no longer going shooting, lest I should yield to the too easy temptation of putting an end to myself with my gun.
> I did not know what I wanted. I was afraid of life; I was driven to leave it; and in spite of that I still hoped something from it.
> All this took place at a time when so far as all my outer circumstances went, I ought to have been completely happy. I had

a good wife who loved me and whom I loved; good children and a large property which was increasing with no pains taken on my part. I was more respected by my kinsfolk and acquaintances than I had ever been; I was loaded with praise by strangers; and without exaggeration I could believe my name already famous. Moreover I was neither insane nor ill. On the contrary, I possessed a physical and mental strength which I have rarely met in persons of my age. I could mow as well as the peasants, I could work with my brain eight hours uninterruptedly and feel no bad effects. . . . What will be the outcome of what I do to-day? Of what I shall do tomorrow? What will be the outcome of all my life? Why should I live? Why should I do anything? Is there in life any purpose which the inevitable death which awaits me does not undo and destroy?

These questions are the simplest in the world. From the stupid child to the wisest old man, they are in the soul of every human being. Without an answer to them, it is impossible, as I experienced, for life to go on.[2]

Tolstoy, fifty years old when he wrote this moving description of his own inner turmoil, could not be considered a healthy personality. And that brings us back to our original question: what is a healthy personality? So far we have only described what it is not. There is a good reason for this; we do not know with certainty what constitutes the healthy personality because there is little agreement among the psychologists working in this field. There are enough definitions of the healthy personality to fill a small book. The best we can accomplish at this stage of our knowledge is to investigate those conceptions of positive psychological health that seem most complete, to see what they tell us about ourselves.

I will discuss the models of the healthy personality proposed by Gordon Allport, Carl Rogers, Erich Fromm, Abraham Maslow, Carl Jung, Viktor Frankl, and Fritz Perls. These theories were selected because they are among the more fully developed and recognized positions and are contemporary in their influence and interest. While not all these theorists are considered growth psychologists, they do propose a level of personality development that is beyond normality and so are in keeping with the spirit of growth psychology.

2. L. Tolstoy, *My Confession* (1882), quoted in W. James, *The Varieties of Religious Experience* (New York: Longmans, Green, 1920), pp. 153–55.

The concept of the healthy personality is vitally important. The content is difficult, challenging, and complex, full of unknowns and half-truths, and no doubt some fad and fancy as well. As such, it reflects the topic it tries to encompass—the human personality.

Many psychologists believe that research on the healthy personality should be the primary focus of psychology; what other discipline investigates the human condition? What entity has more power to change the world, for good or ill, than the human personality? What has more influence on the substance of our lives than the degree of psychological health we bring to bear on our problems?

Abraham Maslow stated the problem clearly: "If you deliberately plan to be less than you are capable of being, then I warn you that you'll be unhappy for the rest of your life."[3]

The purpose of this book is to examine various ways of becoming what we are capable of being.

3. A. H. Maslow, "Neurosis as a Failure of Personal Growth," *Humanitas,* 1967, *3*, 153–69.

2

The mature person
Allport's model

In the summer of 1920, Gordon Allport (1897–1967) met Sigmund Freud. It proved to be an embarrassing but important event for the twenty-three-year-old Allport, for it ultimately led to his rejection of Freudian psychoanalysis in favor of a quite different approach to the study of personality.

Allport was returning to the United States from a year of teaching at Robert College in Istanbul, Turkey, where he had gone after receiving his B.A. from Harvard. He stopped in Vienna to visit one of his brothers, and while there he wrote to Freud with "callow forwardness . . . announcing that I was in Vienna,"[1] implying that Freud would no doubt be glad to meet him.

Freud replied by note with an invitation, which Allport eagerly accepted. On the day of their meeting, Freud ushered Allport into his office and sat down, saying nothing, and waited for Allport to speak. The silence grew longer and Allport became uncomfortable under the intense, steady gaze of the world-famous psychoanalyst.

Finally, desperate for some way to start the conversation, Allport blurted out an incident he had witnessed on the streetcar ride to Freud's home—a four-year-old boy's obvious fear of dirt. The boy believed that everything around him was dirty. Throughout the ride he complained to his mother: "I don't want to sit there." "Don't let that dirty man sit beside me." The mother appeared to Allport to be domineering, extremely neat, and "well starched," and he thought the origin of the boy's dirt phobia was obvious.

There was another silence after Allport finished his story, as Freud continued to stare at the prim and proper young American.

1. G. Allport, *The Person in Psychology* (Boston: Beacon Press, 1968), p. 383.

Then Freud asked, "And was that little boy you?" expressing his belief that whatever people said or did betrayed their own inner conflicts and fears.[2]

Allport was shocked but managed to change the subject. The incident left a deep impression on him, however: it made him become suspicious of the deep probing into the unconscious that was the basis of psychoanalysis. He came away from the experience convinced that psychologists would be better advised to work with a person's surface, or conscious, motives than to plunge into the dark depths of what may lie underneath.[3] This was the path he would follow later in his own studies of personality.

Allport received his Ph.D. from Harvard in 1922 and went on to a distinguished career as the "dean" of American personality study. His work made the study of personality academically respectable in the United States. He had a large, dedicated following of psychologists and received many honors and awards. He was also one of the first psychologists in America to concentrate on the healthy personality instead of the neurotic personality.

ALLPORT'S APPROACH TO PERSONALITY

Allport was more optimistic about human nature than Freud was, and he showed a great compassion for human beings, characteristics that apparently originated in his childhood. His parents stressed the importance of hard work and piety, and they surrounded him with security and affection. Their home was infused with the spirit of humanitarianism, and young Allport was encouraged to seek religious answers to the questions and problems of life. These personal experiences were later reflected in his theoretical views about the nature of personality.

As noted, Allport's personal and professional views were different from those of Freud, and the picture of human nature Allport presented is positive, hopeful, and flattering. One useful approach to understanding Allport's psychological viewpoint, therefore, is to set out the major themes of his theory of personality and to indicate how they differ from Freud's.

Allport did not believe that mature, healthy persons are con-

2. Ibid., pp. 383–84.
3. Some people believe that Freud's question to Allport was full of insight and much to the point. See R. Hogan, *Personality Theory: The Personological Tradition* (Englewood Cliffs, N. J.: Prentice-Hall, 1976), p. 107.

trolled and dominated by unconscious forces—forces they can neither see nor influence. Healthy persons are not driven by unconscious conflicts, nor is their behavior determined by demons deep within them. Allport did believe that unconscious forces are important influences on the behavior of neurotic adults. However, healthy individuals function on a rational and conscious level, fully aware of the forces that guide them, and are able to control those forces as well.

Mature personalities are not controlled by childhood traumas and conflicts. Neurotics are tied, or linked, to childhood experiences, but healthy persons are free of constraints from the past. Mature persons are guided and directed by the present and by their intentions toward, and anticipations of, the future. The outlook of the healthy person is forward, toward contemporary and future events, not backward to childhood events. This healthy perspective offers considerably more freedom of choice and action.

Freud believed that the differences between the neurotic person and the healthy person exist in degree, not in kind; Allport believed that there are no functional similarities at all between the neurotic and the healthy person. Thus, instead of positing a continuum between neurosis and emotional health, Allport suggested a gap, or dichotomy, between the two, with neither type showing any of the characteristics of the other. In Allport's view, the neurotic person operates in the grip of infantile conflicts and experiences and the healthy personality functions on a different and higher plane.

Because he recognized these differences between neurotic and healthy human beings, Allport chose to study only mature adults (in contrast to Freud and others who studied only neurotics) and had little to say about neurotics. Therefore, we can say that Allport's system is definitely health oriented.

THE MOTIVATION OF THE HEALTHY PERSONALITY

Allport believed that the most important problem for the psychologist studying personality is the attempt to explain motivation. What are the forces that push, pull, or in some way direct human actions? Allport felt that the healthy personality is not guided by unconscious forces or childhood experiences. According to Allport, the motives of an adult are not extensions or elaborations of childhood motives. Adult motives are *functionally autonomous* of childhood—that is, they are independent of original circumstances, as autonomous as a full-grown oak tree is of the acorn that once nourished it. We are not pushed from behind by motivating forces with roots in the past. Instead, we are pulled ahead by our plans or intentions for the future.

The central aspect of personality is our deliberate and conscious intentions—hopes, aspirations, and dreams. These goals motivate the mature personality and provide the best clue to understanding present behavior. "The possession of long-range goals, regarded as central to one's personal existence," Allport wrote, "distinguishes the human being from the animal, the adult from the child, and in many cases the healthy personality from the sick."[4]

The *intentional nature* of the healthy personality—this striving toward the future—unifies and integrates the total personality. However beset by problems and conflicts a person may be (and even the healthy personality is not totally free of problems), the personality can, in a sense, be made whole by integrating all its aspects toward the achieving of goals and intentions. Neurotic persons lack long-range purposes and goals, and their personalities become fragmented into unrelated subsystems lacking a central focus or unifying force.

The intentional nature of the personality serves another purpose: it increases the tension level of the individual. Some theories of motivation (including Freud's) assert that human beings are motivated chiefly to reduce tensions, to keep tensions at a minimum and thus maintain a state of internal homeostatic balance, or "homeostasis." In this view individuals are motivated by an excess of tension that they are driven constantly to reduce.

Allport believed that this tension-reduction model of the human personality is only partially correct because it does not account for most of the healthy person's motivation. The human organism needs to maintain a certain level of satisfaction of the biological drives for food, water, sex, and sleep. (Certainly when we are deprived of food the tension induced within us must be reduced.) However, Allport pointed out that the healthy person wants more than tension-reduction out of life. To paraphrase Allport: coming home from work a person is hungry and tired and wants food and rest. But when the person has been replenished and restored, what then? If the person is healthy, he or she wants new activity and turns to a hobby, reads a stimulating book, or goes out for the evening.[5]

Healthy human beings have a continuous need for variety, for new sensations and challenges. They abandon routines and seek out

4. G. Allport, *Becoming: Basic Considerations for a Psychology of Personality* (New Haven: Yale University Press, 1955), p. 51.
5. G. Allport, *Pattern and Growth in Personality* (New York: Holt, Rinehart & Winston, 1961), p. 250.

new experiences. They take risks, gamble, and explore new things. All this activity produces tension. Allport believed, however, that only through these new tension-producing experiences and risks can human beings grow.

History records many individuals who were not content with a routine existence that offered no variety and minimal tension. We all know of people who have quit secure jobs to embark on new careers, who have left their homes to explore and colonize undeveloped lands, who embraced the danger of sky diving or car racing. Why do they do these things? It is not to reduce tensions but to increase them!

Allport wrote about the Polar explorer Roald Amundsen who, from the age of fifteen, was driven solely by the goal of exploration. Amundsen persisted despite great obstacles, and with each successful exploration he raised his level of aspiration. After he discovered the South Pole, he aspired to fly over the North Pole. Amundsen's vision was always toward the future. He was motivated by intentions and dreams. Tension-reduction was certainly not his goal.

Allport believed that the motivation of all healthy persons is identical (although the aspirations and intentions of most of us are probably more modest than those of Amundsen). The healthy person is pulled forward by a vision of the future, and that vision (with its specific goals) unifies the personality and brings the person into contact with increased levels of tension.

It is important to note that nowhere in this discussion of the motivation of the healthy personality have we found happiness as a goal. In Allport's view, happiness is not a goal in itself. Rather, happiness may be a by-product of the successful integration of the personality in its pursuit of aspirations and goals. Happiness is not a major consideration for the healthy person, but it may come to the person who has aspirations and actively pursues them.

Thus, you will be happy to know, it is not necessary to be happy in order to be a mature, healthy person. The healthy personality is not necessarily the happy-go-lucky, euphoric personality. In fact, Allport believed that it is possible for a healthy person's life to be grim and filled with pain and sorrow.

There is another aspect of Allport's conception of the healthy personality that may seem paradoxical: the goals to which the healthy person aspires are, in the final analysis, unattainable! He seems to suggest that while immediate subgoals are attainable, the ultimate goal is not. For example, no matter how successful the explorer Amundsen was in his various journeys, his exploration goal could never be fully satisfied. After each new discovery (the satisfaction of a subgoal) he immediately began planning for the next. His life was directed (motivated) by the overall goal of continuing exploration, but this goal could never be fully satisfied so long as there were any unexplored territories.

We are reminded of the saying "The more you get, the more you want." The ultimate goal pulls the person from one subgoal to another, but it remains always in the future, out of reach, until death or some equally insurmountable obstacle intervenes.[6]

We've all heard someone say "If I could make $15,000 a year, I'd be satisfied. I wouldn't need any more." Very likely that person will find that when the stated goal is reached, he or she won't be satisfied; then a higher income level becomes a new goal. The ultimate goal of a sufficient income may never be attained and the person is pulled to ever-higher levels of achievement. Allport wrote: "Salvation comes only to him who ceaselessly bestirs himself in the pursuit of objectives that in the end are not fully attained."[7]

Perhaps it is fortunate that our ultimate goals are never fully reached, for what would happen if they were? We would no longer have a motivating force to direct our lives and to integrate and unify all aspects of our personalities. We would have to develop a new motive to take the place of the old one in order for the personality to remain healthy.

Allport recognized this need to invent motives if existing ones turn out to be insufficient or no longer appropriate, and so he proposed the *principle of organizing the energy level*. The mature, healthy person constantly needs motives of sufficient strength and vitality to consume his or her energies. For example, a woman may have as her overriding goal the raising of her children in accordance with her criteria of what is proper. When the children are young and are growing toward maturity, this goal is sufficient to consume her energy. She may achieve subgoals along the way—such as toilet training the children or easing their adjustment to school—as the children successfully reach various stages of development. But what happens when the children reach adulthood? There is nothing more for the woman to do; in this case the goal has been outgrown. She must find new interests and dreams. Her energy must be redirected.

Allport applied the same reasoning to the problem of teenage vandalism, crime, and rebellion. He believed that some young people lack meaningful, constructive goals to consume their energy. The

6. Amundsen died while trying to rescue another explorer.
7. G. Allport, *Becoming* (New Haven: Yale University Press, 1955), p. 67.

energy must find an outlet, and if it is not expressed in a constructive way it may be released in a destructive way.

Allport's theory of motivation of the healthy personality also includes the *principle of mastery and competence,* which holds that it is not sufficiently satisfying for mature, healthy persons to perform or achieve at mediocre or merely adequate levels. Rather, they are driven to perform as well as they possibly can, to attain high levels of competence and mastery in striving to satisfy their motives.

As you can see, motivation (of a constructive sort) is vital for psychologically healthy persons. Such persons actively pursue goals, hopes, and dreams, and their lives are guided by a sense of purpose, dedication, and commitment. The pursuit of a goal never ends; if a goal must be discarded, a new motive must be formed quickly. Healthy persons look to and live in the future.

THE SELF OF THE HEALTHY PERSON

The concept of *self* is an important part of any discussion of the healthy personality. Both the word and the concept seem simple until we begin to examine the diverse ways in which personality theorists attempt to explain its nature and function. The variety of explanations is likely to leave us with a sense of bewilderment about what this simple term might mean.

The Proprium

Allport hoped to eliminate the contradictions and ambiguities inherent in discussions of the self by eliminating the word and substituting for it one that would distinguish his concept of self from all the others. The term he chose is *proprium,* and it can be defined by considering the adjective form "propriate," as in the word "appropriate." *Proprium* refers to something that belongs to or is unique to a person. It follows that the proprium (or self) is composed of those matters and processes that are important and personal to an individual, those aspects that define a person as unique. Allport called it "the me as felt and known."[8]

8. G. Allport, *Pattern and Growth in Personality* (New York: Holt, Rinehart & Winston, 1961), p. 127.

Development of the Proprium

The proprium develops from infancy to adolescence through seven stages of selfhood. When all the developmental aspects have fully emerged, they are united in the single concept of the proprium. Thus, the proprium is the composite of these seven aspects of selfhood. The emergence of the proprium is a requisite for a healthy personality.

Bodily Self.   We are not born with a sense of self; it is not part of our genetic endowment. The infant is not able to distinguish between self ("me") and the world around it. Gradually, through increasingly complex learning and perceptual experiences, a vague distinction develops between something "in me" and other things "out there." As the infant touches, sees, and hears itself, other people, and objects, the distinction becomes clearer. At about the age of 15 months, the first stage in the development of the proprium emerges—the *bodily self*.

This awareness of a "bodily me"—for example, the infant's distinguishing between its fingers and an object held in its fingers—is the first step toward achieving total selfhood. Allport called it "a lifelong anchor for our self-awareness,"[9] although it is far from being the person's total self.

Self-identity.   In the second stage of development the sense of *self-identity* emerges. The child becomes aware of its continuing identity as a separate person. The child learns its name, realizes that the reflection in the mirror today is of the same person as the one seen yesterday, and believes that the sense of "me," or self, persists in the face of changing experiences.

Allport felt that the most important aspect of self-identity is a person's name. It becomes the symbol of one's existence, identifying one's self and distinguishing it from all the other selves in the world.

Self-esteem.   The third stage in the development of the proprium is the emergence of *self-esteem*. This is concerned with the child's feeling of pride as a result of learning to do things on its own. At this stage the child wants to make things, to explore and satisfy its curiosity about the environment, and to manipulate and change that environment. The curious and aggressive two-year-old child can be

9.   Ibid., p. 114.

very destructive as this urge to manipulate and explore takes hold. Allport believed this to be a crucial stage of development; if parents frustrate the child's need to explore, the emerging sense of self-esteem may be damaged. Feelings of humiliation and anger can result.

Central to the emergence of self-esteem is the child's need for autonomy. This manifests itself in negative behavior around the age of two, when the child seems to oppose virtually everything the parents want it to do. Later, by age six or seven, self-esteem is defined more in terms of competitiveness with one's peers.

Self-extension.   The next stage of development, *self-extension,* begins around age four. The child has become aware of other people and objects in the environment and of the fact that some of them belong to the child. The child speaks of "my house" or "my school." The child is learning the meaning and value of possessiveness as embodied in that marvelous word "mine." While at this age the circle of objects and people identified as "mine" is limited, the process by which larger entities (such as country, career, or religion) become "mine" is now established. This is the beginning of the person's ability to extend his or her self broadly to include not only things but also abstractions, values, and beliefs.

Self-image.   The *self-image* develops next. This refers to how the child sees itself, the opinion it holds of itself. This image (or series of images) develops from interactions between the parents and the child. Through praise and punishment, the child learns that its parents expect it to display certain behaviors and avoid others. Parents may call the child "good" in response to some behaviors and "bad" in response to others. By learning these parental expectations, the child develops the foundation for a sense of moral responsibility and for the formulation of goals and intentions.

The Self as a Rational Coper.   After the child begins school, the *self as a rational coper* begins to emerge. New rules and expectations are learned from teachers and schoolmates and, more importantly, intellectual activities and challenges are presented. The child learns that it can solve problems by the use of logic and rational processes.

Propriate Striving.   In adolescence, *propriate striving*—the last stage in the development of selfhood—appears. Allport believed that adolescence is a particularly crucial time. The person is engaged in a renewed quest for self-identity, quite different from the one at age two. The question "Who am I?" is paramount. Pushed and pulled in different directions by parents and peers, the adolescent experiments with masks and roles, testing the self-image, trying to find an adult personality. The most important aspect of this search for identity is the definition of a life-goal. The significance of this search is that for the first time the person is concerned with the future, with long-range goals and dreams.

Concurrent with this is the development of the forward thrust of motivation. The person's intentions, aspirations, and hopes motivate the mature personality. These "defining objectives," in Allport's terms, are vital to the healthy personality.

These seven stages of the self, or proprium, unfold from infancy to adolescence. An overwhelming failure or frustration at any one stage cripples the emergence of later stages and hinders their harmonious integration in the proprium. Childhood experiences, then, are extremely important in the development of the healthy personality.

THE DEVELOPMENT OF THE HEALTHY PERSONALITY

Allport did not describe the development of personality in terms of clear-cut stages, as he did the development of the self. This relative inattention to personality development is in keeping with his belief that the adult personality is more a function of a person's present and future than of his or her past. Only with the neurotic is there a functionally continuous relationship between the child and the adult. Nevertheless, Allport did describe certain childhood experiences that differ between neurotic and healthy persons, and it is worthwhile to explore them briefly.

Allport was concerned with the relationship between the infant and its mother, especially with the amount of security and affection she provides to the child. If the infant receives sufficient security and affection, positive psychological growth will ensue throughout the seven stages of the self's emergence. The child will form an identity and a self-image, and the self will begin to extend beyond the person. During adolescence, propriate strivings will form to provide a frame of reference and motivation for future growth. With all aspects of the self in place, a healthy, mature adult will almost inevitably emerge.

Obviously, then, the role of the mother is of great importance. What happens if she does not supply sufficient security and affection to the infant? A child raised under these conditions becomes insecure, aggressive, demanding, jealous, and self-centered, and psychological growth is minimized. As an adult, the person will be controlled by childhood motivations and by infantile drives and conflicts, and is likely to develop some form of mental illness.

Allport was vague on the crucial question whether a person, under some circumstances, might be able to counteract unfortunate early childhood experiences. Could the effects of a rejecting mother be overcome by a sympathetic teacher, a caring older relative, or, later in life, by the love of a spouse? Or is such a person doomed to neurosis? It would be comforting to believe that satisfaction later in life of thwarted childhood needs for security and affection will compensate for the early setbacks, but this possibility was not made clear by Allport. He had little to say about neurotic behavior, since he was much more interested in the healthy personality.

CRITERIA OF THE MATURE PERSONALITY

These seven criteria of maturity represent Allport's views on specific characteristics of the healthy personality.

1. Extension of the Sense of Self

As the self develops, it extends to a widening range of people and objects. At first the self is focused solely on the individual. Then, as the circle of experience grows, the self broadens to include abstract values and ideals. In other words, as the person matures, he or she develops interests outside of the self. However, it is not sufficient merely to interact with something or someone beyond the self, such as a job. The person must become a direct and full participant. Allport called this "authentic participation by the person in some significant spheres of human endeavor."[10] The person must extend the self *into* the activity.

We know that it is possible to work actively at something (such as a college course or a job) without feeling a genuine personal involvement or a sense of participation. In Allport's view, an activity must be relevant and important to the self; it must mean something to the person. If you work at a job because you believe it is important, be-

10.   Ibid., pp. 283–84.

cause it challenges your abilities, or because doing it to the best of your ability makes you feel good, then you are a genuine participant in that job. The activity means more to you than the income derived; it satisfies other needs as well.

The more a person is fully involved with various activities or people or ideas, the more psychologically healthy he or she will be. This sense of authentic participation applies to our work, our relationships with family and friends, our hobbies, and our political or religious affiliations. The self becomes invested in these meaningful activities and they become extensions of the sense of self.

2.   Warm Relating of Self to Others

Allport distinguished two kinds of warmth in relation to other people: the capacity for intimacy and the capacity for compassion.

The psychologically healthy person is capable of displaying intimacy (love) for a parent, child, spouse, or close friend. What brings forth this capacity for intimacy is a well-developed sense of self-extension. The person manifests authentic participation with the loved one and a concern for his or her welfare; this becomes as important as the individual's own welfare. Another requisite for the capacity for intimacy is a well-developed sense of self-identity.

There is a difference between the love relationships of neurotics and those of healthy personalities. Neurotics need to receive love much more than they are able to give it. When they do give love, it is with conditions and obligations that are not reciprocated. The love of healthy persons is unconditional, not crippling or binding.

Compassion, the second kind of warmth, involves an understanding of the basic human condition and a sense of kinship with all peoples. The healthy person has the capacity to understand the pains, passions, fears, and failures that characterize human existence. This empathy comes about through an "imaginative extension" of one's own feelings to humanity at large.

As a result of the capacity for compassion, the mature personality is tolerant of other people's behavior and does not judge or condemn. The healthy person accepts human frailties, knowing that he or she shares the same weaknesses. The neurotic, however, is intolerant and incapable of understanding the universality of basic human experiences.

3. Emotional Security

This characteristic of the healthy personality includes several qualities; the major one is self-acceptance. Healthy personalities are capable of accepting all aspects of their being, including weaknesses and failings, without being passively resigned to them. For example, mature persons can accept their sex drive without becoming excessively prudish or repressed, as neurotics may become. Mature persons are capable of living with this and other aspects of human nature with little conflict within themselves or with society. They try to do the best they can, and in the process, try to improve themselves.

Mature personalities also are capable of accepting human emotions; they are not prisoners of their emotions, nor do they try to hide from them. Healthy personalities control their emotions so that these do not disrupt interpersonal activities. This control is not repression, but rather a redirecting of the emotions into more constructive channels. Neurotics, however, give way to whatever emotion is dominant at the moment, frequently displaying anger or hatred, no matter how inappropriate these feelings might be.

Another quality of emotional security is what Allport called "frustration tolerance." This indicates how a person reacts to stress and to the thwarting of wants and desires. Healthy persons tolerate these setbacks; they do not resign themselves to frustration but instead are capable of devising different, less frustrating, ways of reaching the same or substitute goals. Frustrations are not crippling to healthy personalities as they often are to neurotics.

Mature persons could not be so tolerant of frustration, so self-accepting, or so much in control of their emotions if they did not feel a basic sense of security. They have learned to deal with life's fears and ego-threats with a sense of proportion, and they have found that such stresses do not always lead to disaster. Healthy persons are not free of insecurities and fears, but they feel less threatened and better able to cope with them than do neurotics.

4. Realistic Perception

Healthy persons regard their world objectively. Neurotics, in contrast, must often distort reality in order to make it compatible with their own wants, needs, and fears. Mature persons do not need to believe that other people or situations are all evil or all good in accordance with a personal preconception of reality. They accept reality for what it is.

5.   Skills and Assignments

Allport was emphatic about the importance of work and the necessity for losing oneself in it. Success at work implies the development of certain skills and abilities—a level of competence. But it is not sufficient to possess the relevant skills; we must use them in a wholehearted, enthusiastic, committed manner and invest the self fully in our work.

Allport noted that it is possible for persons who do possess skills to be neurotic. However, it is not possible to find healthy, mature persons who have not directed their skills toward their work. So strong is this commitment in healthy persons that they are able to submerge all ego-related defenses and drives (such as pride) while they are absorbed in their work. This dedication to work is related to the notion of responsibility and to a positive survival of life. Allport quoted the famous brain surgeon Harvey Cushing on this point: "The only way to endure life is to have a task to complete."[11]

Work and responsibility provide meaning and a sense of continuity to life. It is not possible to achieve maturity and positive psychological health without having important work to do and the dedication, commitment, and skills with which to do it.

6.   Self-objectification

This criterion is embodied in the old prescription "Know thyself"—certainly a difficult task. The search for objective self-knowledge begins early in life and never ceases, but it is possible to attain a certain useful level of self-objectification at any age. The healthy personality achieves a higher level of self-understanding than does the neurotic.

Adequate knowledge of one's self requires insight into the relationship between what one thinks one is and what one actually is. The closer the correspondence between these two ideas, the greater is the individual's maturity. Another important relationship is between what one thinks one is and what others think one is. The healthy person is open to the opinions of others in formulating an objective picture of his or her self.

The person who possesses a high level of self-objectification, or self-insight, is not likely to project personal negative qualities onto other people. The person tends to be an accurate judge of others and

11.   Ibid., p. 290.

is usually better accepted by others. Allport also suggested that the person who possesses greater self-insight is more intelligent than the person who possesses less self-insight.

In addition, although you may laugh at the idea, there is a high correlation between level of self-insight and sense of humor, the kind of humor that involves the perception of incongruities and absurdities and the ability to laugh at oneself. (Allport distinguished this from crude comic humor dealing with sex and aggression.)

7. A Unifying Philosophy of Life

Healthy personalities are forward-looking, motivated by long-range goals and plans. These persons have a sense of purpose, a mission to work at accomplishing, as the cornerstone of their lives, and this supplies continuity to their personalities.

Allport called this unifying motivation *directedness,* and it is more evident in healthy personalities than in neurotics. Directedness guides all aspects of a person's life toward a goal (or series of goals) and gives the person a reason for living. We need the constant pull of meaningful goals; without them, we are likely to experience personality problems. Thus, to Allport it seemed impossible to have a healthy personality without aspirations and direction toward the future.

Perhaps the framework for specific goals is the idea of *values.* Values (along with goals), Allport emphasized, are vital to the development of a unifying philosophy of life. An individual may choose among a variety of values and they may be related to one's self (such as pride in individual workmanship) or they may be broad and shared by many others (such as patriotism).

The possession of strong values clearly separates the healthy person from the neurotic. The neurotic either has no values or only fragmentary and transient values. The neurotic's values are not permanent or strong enough to link or unify all aspects of life.

The attribute of *conscience* contributes to a unifying philosophy of life. Allport noted the difference between a mature conscience and an immature or neurotic one. An immature conscience is like a child's, obedient and slavish, full of restrictions and prohibitions carried from childhood into adulthood. It is characterized by the feeling of "must" rather than "ought." In other words, the immature person says, "I must behave this way"; the mature person says, "I ought to behave this way." The mature conscience consists of a sense of duty and responsibility to itself and to others, and may be rooted in religious or ethical values.

A PERSONAL COMMENT

Several aspects of Allport's approach to the human personality are original. He was the first personality theorist to study mature, normal adults instead of neurotics. Freud and other early theorists developed their theories on the basis of observations of disturbed personalities. As a result, their theories focus largely on neuroses. Allport studied normal individuals and so developed a theory concerned almost entirely with the healthy personality.

Allport theorized a gap between the neurotic and the healthy personality and between adulthood and childhood. He remains the only personality theorist to assert that there are no functional similarities between disturbed and healthy personalities, that they are separate entities.

There is a similar functional separation between the child and the healthy adult. Freud and other personality theorists viewed all human beings as products (or prisoners) of childhood experiences, but Allport believed that this is true only for neurotics. He did not deny the importance of childhood influences—indeed, they can spell the difference between neurosis and psychological health—but the healthy personality, once formed, is free of the past.

Psychological health, therefore, is forward-looking, not backward-looking. The outlook is toward what the person hopes to become, not to what has already happened and cannot be changed. This seems to me to make Allport's view of personality very hopeful and optimistic. The future can consciously and deliberately be planned for and worked toward for the betterment of the individual. A life that focuses on the past, however, is not so open to change.

I find the idea of a future orientation—the focus on long-range goals, purposes, and dreams—to be an agreeable one. Clearly it seems healthier to anticipate, plan, and strive, than to dwell in the events of the past. Also, Allport's focus on the necessity of increasing rather than decreasing the tension level agrees with my own experience and knowledge of the lives of historical figures. Vital, active human beings need diversity in their lives; they are not content with routine. We all know persons who gamble and take chances, who actively seek stimulation and challenge in their lives.

And when we satisfy each dream and reach each goal on the path to the ultimate goal, we (those of us who think we are mature, healthy personalities) actively seek new motives and goals. What provides excitement and zest in life is the chase more than the capture, the achieving more than the achievement, the striving more than the success.

Anticipations are prominent in Allport's theory in helping us define who and what we are, in shaping our self-identity. This is like saying, "I am what I strive to be." This emphasis on what we hope to become is echoed by other theorists in this book, and I wholeheartedly agree with this notion.

Another aspect of Allport's view of psychological health, which other theorists repeat, is that healthy personalities are directed toward other people. Far from being totally self-centered, the mature person is actively involved, committed to something or someone beyond the self. The person is not a passive spectator of life, isolated and withdrawn, but is fully and vitally immersed in life. Meaningful work is a necessity and so is the well-being of another person, a loved one or the larger community of fellow human beings. The healthy person is able to love and extend the self into deeply caring relationships with others; the growth and fulfillment of others becomes at least as important as his or her own growth and development.

These are highly realistic persons. They know themselves, and they accept their limitations and are not beaten by them. Simply stated, mature persons know who they are and they are therefore secure in their relationships with themselves and with the world around them.

There is, to me, a commonsense appeal to these characteristics. Many of Allport's prescriptions for a mature, healthy personality seem to be a distillation of the basic truths philosophers and theologians have been preaching for centuries. It seems obvious that it is healthy to have a firm self-image and self-identity, to feel a sense of self-esteem, to be able to give love openly and unconditionally, to feel emotionally secure, and to have goals and a sense of purpose that give meaning and direction to life.

In a sense, perhaps Allport has not told us anything we did not already know. Perhaps he is restating old bromides. But there is nothing wrong with a refreshing dose of old bromides, if only to remind us that they may contain kernels of truth. (Bromides that contain no element of truth usually do not become old, and so are not passed on to succeeding generations, as many of Allport's prescriptions have been.) And, as we shall see, some of these basic truths are offered by other theorists as well.

Allport's strength was his ability to perceive common themes in the lives of psychologically healthy persons and to state those themes with a clarity that is rare among psychologists. That he may have offered timeless truths is supported by our knowledge of the lives of historical and contemporary men and women who have exhibited the characteristics and attributes which he described so forcefully. Whether Allport has given us the complete description of the healthy personality cannot be decided until we examine other models of psychological health, which add additional dimensions to Allport's portrait of the mature, healthy person.

BIBLIOGRAPHY

Allport, G. *Becoming: Basic Considerations for a Psychology of Personality.* New Haven: Yale University Press, 1955.

——. *Personality and Social Encounter.* Boston: Beacon Press, 1960.

——. *Pattern and Growth in Personality.* New York: Holt, Rinehart & Winston, 1961.

——. Autobiography. In E. G. Boring & G. Lindzey (eds.), *History of Psychology in Autobiography,* Vol. 5. New York: Appleton-Century-Crofts, 1967.

——. *The Person in Psychology.* Boston: Beacon Press, 1968.

Maddi, S. R., and Costa, P. T. *Humanism in Personology: Allport, Maslow, and Murray.* Chicago: Aldine-Atherton, 1972.

3

The fully functioning person
Rogers' model

In Peking, China, in 1922, twenty-year-old Carl Rogers (1902–) underwent an experience that would shape the form and substance of his approach to personality. During a six-month sojourn as a delegate to an international Christian student conference, important changes took place within him. He came home from China for his junior year at the University of Wisconsin a different person with a new life-theme that would be reflected in his personal and professional life.

Rogers' upbringing was characterized by strict and uncompromising fundamentalist Christianity, with an emphasis on proper moral behavior and the virtue of hard work. The religious teachings of his parents held him in a firm grip throughout boyhood and adolescence and were not loosened when he entered college. Indeed, he resolved in his sophomore year to devote his life to "Christian work" by becoming a minister.

The following year Rogers was chosen to attend the World Student Christian Federation Conference in China. It opened up his world in many ways. He found an important and new part of himself in his journey to the other side of the world. For the first time he was exposed to people of diverse intellectual and cultural backgrounds, whose ideas were as foreign to him as were their appearance and language. As he talked with the other student delegates, he began to be affected by their ideas. His bedrock fundamentalist beliefs were penetrated, weakened, and finally discarded.

Rogers recorded his thoughts and feelings at that time in a journal. He sent one copy of it to the girl he would later marry and another copy to his parents. He continued to record and send his

24

thoughts as the weeks stretched into months. At home, his parents grew increasingly alarmed by each long letter, but Rogers knew nothing of the trouble he was causing because of the delay in receiving mail from the United States. It was two months before his parents' reaction to the first letter reached him.

The result of Rogers' experiences in China was the breaking of religious and intellectual ties with his parents and the realization that he "could think my own thoughts, come to my own conclusions, and take the stands I believed in."[1] This newly achieved freedom, and the sense of confidence and direction it provided, led him to realize that ultimately a person must rely only on his or her own experience. That belief and trust in one's own experience became the cornerstone of Rogers' approach to personality.

Rogers received his Ph.D. from Columbia University Teachers College in 1931 and went on to become prominent for his development of nondirective, or client-centered, therapy. This form of therapy is very popular in the United States and has been used to attempt to improve the human personality in a variety of settings.

Rogers' approach to therapy, and the model of the healthy personality which derived from it, provides a flattering and optimistic picture of human nature. His major theme is a reflection of what he learned about himself at age twenty: that a person must rely on his or her own experience of the world, for that is the only reality an individual can know.

ROGERS' APPROACH TO PERSONALITY

Unlike Allport, whose data derived solely from the study of mature, healthy adults, Rogers worked with disturbed individuals who sought help in changing their personalities. To treat these patients (he prefers to call them "clients"), Rogers developed a method of therapy which places the major responsibility for personality change on the client, not on the therapist (as in Freud's approach). Thus, the term *client-centered therapy*. Obviously, this method assumes that the disturbed individual possesses a certain level of ability and awareness, and it tells us much about Rogers' view of human nature.

If persons are responsible for and capable of improving their own personalities, then they must be conscious and rational beings.

1. C. R. Rogers, "Autobiography," in E. G. Boring and G. Lindzey, eds., *History of Psychology in Autobiography,* Vol. 5 (New York: Appleton-Century-Crofts, 1967), p. 351.

Rogers believes that people are guided by their own conscious perception of their selves and the world around them, not by unconscious forces which they cannot control. A person's ultimate criterion is his on her own conscious experience, and that experience provides the intellectual and emotional framework within which the personality continually grows.

According to Rogers, we rational, conscious human beings are not controlled by childhood events such as toilet training, early weaning, or premature sex experiences. These do not doom or damn us to lives of conflict and anxiety over which we have no control. The present, and how we perceive it, is for the healthy personality of much greater importance than the past. However, Rogers notes that past experiences can influence the way in which we perceive the present, which, in turn, influences our level of psychological health. Thus, childhood experiences are important, but Rogers' focus remains on what is happening to us now, not what happened then.

In his work with clients, Rogers held that personality must be examined and understood through the client's personal viewpoint, his or her own subjective experiences. Just as in his personal life Rogers came to trust his own experiences, so in his professional life he came to trust his clients' experiences. What is real for each client is his or her unique perception of reality.

Rogers believes that since this reality is subject to each person's perceptual experiences, it will differ from one person to another. Nevertheless, he argues for a common, basic motivational force: the tendency or striving to actualize.

THE MOTIVATION OF THE HEALTHY PERSON: ACTUALIZATION

Rogers posits a single motivation—"one fundamental need"—in his system of personality: to maintain, actualize, and enhance all aspects of the individual. This tendency is innate and encompasses physiological and psychological components of growth, although, during the early years of life, it is more oriented toward physiological aspects.

No aspect of human growth and development operates independently of this actualizing tendency. At the lower levels, the actualizing tendency is responsible for basic physiological needs for food, water, and air. It therefore enables the organism to survive by sustaining and maintaining basic bodily needs.

Actualization does much more than maintain the organism, however; it also facilitates and enhances maturation and growth. As the infant grows, the body's organs and physiological processes become increasingly complex and differentiated as they begin to function in their intended ways. This maturation process ranges from changes in the size and form of the newborn to the development of secondary sex characteristics at puberty.

The achievement of full maturation is not automatic, despite the fact that the "blueprints" for the maturation process are contained in the individual's genetic structure. The process requires much effort; Rogers compares it with the struggle and pain involved when a child learns to walk. The child stumbles and falls and hurts itself. It would be easier and less painful to stop trying to stand and take those first steps. Yet the child continues to try and eventually succeeds. Why does the child persist? Rogers feels that the tendency to actualize, as a motivating force, is much stronger than the pain and struggle and any accompanying urge to cease the effort to develop.

The actualizing tendency at the physiological level is virtually irresistible; it thrusts the individual forward from one stage of maturation to the next, compelling him or her to adapt and to grow.[2]

As you can see, this physiological aspect of the actualizing tendency is not oriented toward the reduction of tension. The struggle and tenacity involved in actualization bring us into contact with more, not less, tension. The goal of life, then, is not simply the maintenance of a homeostatic balance or a high degree of ease and comfort, but growth and enhancement. Our direction is forward, toward the goal of increased complexity of functioning, so that we may become all that we are capable of becoming.

At this biological level, Rogers makes no distinction between healthy and nonhealthy human beings. Apparently he found no differences between the emotionally well and the emotionally ill in terms of the amount or rate of what might be called biological actualization. But when we consider psychological aspects of actualization, differences do appear.

As a person grows older, the self begins to develop. At the same time, the emphasis in actualization is shifting from physiological to

2. Rogers believes that this aspect of the actualizing tendency is found in all living things. Animals, trees, and even seaweed possess it, as Rogers described in poetic fashion: "Here in this palmlike seaweed was the tenacity of life, the forward thrust of life, the ability to push into an incredibly hostile environment and not only hold its own, but to adapt, develop, become itself." C. R. Rogers, "Actualizing tendency in relation to motives and to consciousness," in M. R. Jones, ed., *Nebraska Symposium on Motivation, 1963* (Lincoln: University of Nebraska Press, 1963), p. 2.

psychological. The body, and its specific forms and functions, has reached its adult level of development, and growth is then concentrated on the personality. Rogers does not make clear when this transformation takes place, but one might infer from his writings that it begins in childhood and is completed in late adolescence.

Once the self begins to emerge, the tendency toward *self-actualization* appears. This life-long, continuing process is the most important goal in a person's life. Self-actualization is the process of becoming oneself, of developing one's unique psychological characteristics and potentialities. Rogers believes that humans have an innate urge to create and that the most important creative product is one's own self, a goal achieved much more often by healthy persons than by psychologically ill ones.

There is one important difference between the general tendency toward actualization and the specific tendency toward self-actualization. The maturation and development of the total organism is not greatly influenced by learning and experience. For example, assuming proper hormonal/chemical functioning, a person will develop the secondary sex characteristics; experience has nothing to do with this kind of development. The actualization of the self, however, is determined by social rather than biological forces. Thus, self-actualization will be aided or hindered by experience and by learning, particularly in childhood.

THE DEVELOPMENT OF THE SELF

In infancy the child begins to differentiate, or separate, one aspect of its experience from all the rest. This aspect is the self and it is represented by increasing use of the words "me" and "mine." The infant develops the ability to discriminate between what belongs to or is part of itself and all the other objects it sees, hears, touches, and smells as it begins to form a picture and image of who it is. In other words, the child develops a self-concept.

As part of the self-concept, the child also pictures who it should be or might like to be. Such images are formed as a result of increasingly complex interactions with other people. By perceiving the reactions of other persons to its own behavior, the infant develops, ideally, a consistent pattern of self-images, an integrated whole in which any possible incongruities between the self as it exists and the self as it might want to be are minimized. In the healthy, self-actualizing individual, a coherent pattern emerges. The situation is different for an emotionally disturbed individual.

The specific ways in which the self develops, and whether or not it will turn out to be healthy, depend on the love the child receives in infancy. At the time the self is beginning to develop, the infant also learns to need love; Rogers calls this need *positive regard.*

Positive regard, a compelling and pervasive need, is possessed by all human beings; every infant is driven to seek positive regard. However, not every infant will find sufficient satisfaction of this need. It is satisfying for the infant to receive affection, love, and approval from other people,[3] but it is frustrating to receive disapproval and a lack of love and affection. Whether the infant will grow to become a healthy personality, then, depends on how well this need for positive regard is satisfied.

The developing self-concept of the infant is greatly influenced by the mother. What if she does not bestow positive regard on the child? What if she is disapproving and rejecting of her child's behavior? The infant perceives any disapproval (even if it focuses on only one aspect of behavior) as a broad, diffuse disapproval of every aspect of its being. The infant becomes sensitive to any sign of rejection and soon begins to plan its behavior on the basis of the reaction it is expected to bring.

In this case, the child looks to others, not to itself, for guidance about its behavior. The need for positive regard, stronger now that it has been frustrated, takes up more and more energy and thought. The child must work hard for positive regard at the expense of actualization of the self.

The infant in this situation develops what Rogers calls *conditional positive regard.* The affection and love the child receives are conditional upon its proper behavior. As the infant is developing conditional positive regard, it is internalizing the mother's attitudes. When that happens, the attitudes of the mother are taken over by the child and applied to itself.

For example, if the mother expresses disapproval every time an infant drops an object out of its crib, the infant eventually comes to disapprove of itself whenever it behaves in that way. External standards of judgment have become its own, and the child "punishes" itself as the mother did earlier. The child "loves" itself only when it behaves in ways it knows the mother approves. Thus, the self becomes a "mother-surrogate."

Out of this sorry state of affairs in which the infant receives conditional positive regard first from the mother and then from itself, *conditions of worth* develop. This means that the infant feels a sense of

3. At this age, "other people" usually means the mother.

self-worth only under certain conditions. The infant must avoid behaving or thinking in those ways which bring disapproval and rejection by standards the child has adopted from the mother. Performing
forbidden behaviors causes the infant to feel guilty and unworthy,
conditions which the infant must then defend against. And so defensiveness becomes part of the child's behavior. It is activated whenever
anxiety occurs; that is, whenever the child, and later the adult, is
tempted to display the forbidden type of behavior. As a result of this
defensiveness, the individual's freedom is limited; his or her true nature or self cannot be fully expressed.

The self is not allowed to fully actualize because certain of its
aspects must be held in check. Conditions of worth act like blinders on
a horse, cutting off a portion of the available experience. Persons with
conditions of worth must limit their behavior and distort reality because even becoming aware of unworthy behaviors and thoughts can
be as threatening as displaying them. Since these individuals cannot
interact fully and openly with their environment, they develop what
Rogers calls *incongruence* between the concept of self and the reality
that surrounds them. They cannot actualize all aspects of the self. In
other words, they cannot develop healthy personalities.

We have discussed how the person who is not psychologically
healthy develops. Let us now note the not surprisingly opposite conditions of childhood which foster the development of psychological
health.

The primary requisite for the emergence of a healthy personality is the receipt of *unconditional positive regard* in infancy. This
develops when the mother bestows love and affection regardless of
how the child behaves. This freely given love and affection, and the
attitude it represents, become an internalized set of norms and standards for the infant, just as the attitudes of the mother displaying conditional positive regard were internalized by her infant.

Unconditional positive regard does not require the absence of all
restraints on the child's behavior; it does not mean that the infant is
allowed to do whatever it wants without being admonished. If this
were true, the mother might not protect her child from dangers—for
example, pulling the child away from a hot stove—for fear of making
her positive regard conditional.

Rogers believes that the mother can disapprove of certain behaviors without at the same time establishing conditions under which
the child will receive love and affection. This can be accomplished in
an atmosphere which fosters the infant's acceptance of the unde-
sirability of some behaviors without its being made to feel guilty and

unworthy at having performed them. It is not so much being admonished that can set up conditions of worth for the child as it is the way in which the admonishment is administered.

Children who grow up with the feeling of unconditional positive regard will not develop conditions of worth. They feel themselves worthy under all conditions. And, if there are no conditions of worth, then there is no need for defensive behavior. There will be no incongruence between the self and the perception of reality.

No experience is threatening to such a person; he or she is able to partake of life freely and fully. The self is deep and broad because it contains all the thoughts and feelings the person is capable of expressing. It is also flexible and open to all new experiences. No part of the self is crippled or thwarted in its expression.

This person is free to become self-actualizing, to develop all of his or her potential. And once the process of self-actualization is underway, the person is able to proceed toward the ultimate goal, becoming a fully functioning person.

THE FULLY FUNCTIONING PERSON

The first point to note about Rogers' version of the healthy personality is that it is not a state of being but a *process*, "a direction, not a destination."[4] Self-actualizing is ongoing; it is never a finished or static condition. This goal, this future orientation, pulls the individual ahead, further differentiating and developing all aspects of the self. Rogers called one of his books *On Becoming a Person;* this aptly summarizes the continuing nature of the process.

The second point about self-actualization is that it is a difficult and at times painful process. It involves a continuous testing, stretching, and prodding of all a person's capabilities. "It involves the courage to be," Rogers wrote. "It means launching oneself fully into the stream of life."[5] Such a person is immersed in and open to the full range of human emotions and experiences and feels these far more deeply than a less healthy person.

Rogers does not describe self-actualizing persons as happy or contented all or even much of the time, although they do experience these feelings. As Allport does, Rogers looks upon happiness as a by-product of the striving for self-actualization; happiness is not a goal in

4. C. R. Rogers, *On Becoming a Person: A Therapist's View of Psychotherapy* (Boston: Houghton Mifflin, 1961), p. 186.
5. Ibid., p. 196.

itself. Self-actualizing persons lead lives that are enriching, challenging, and meaningful, but they do not necessarily laugh all the time.

A third point about self-actualizing persons is that they are truly themselves. They do not hide behind masks or facades, pretending to be something they are not or shielding a part of their selves. They do not follow behavioral prescriptions or display different personalities for different situations. They are free of expectations and inhibitions imposed by their society or their parents; they have outgrown these rules. Rogers does not believe that self-actualizing persons live under codes laid down by others. The direction chosen, the behavior displayed, is determined solely by the individuals themselves. The self is the master of the personality and it operates independently of the norms prescribed by others. However, self-actualizing persons are not openly aggressive, rebellious, or deliberately unconventional in flouting the rules of parents or of society. They recognize that they can function as individuals within the broad sanctions and guidelines of society.

In addition to these general comments, Rogers offers five specific characteristics of the fully functioning person.

1. An Openness to Experience

A person with no inhibiting conditions of worth is free to experience all feelings and attitudes. None has to be defended against, for none is threatening. Openness to experience is thus the opposite of defensiveness. Every sensation and feeling, of internal and external origin, is relayed to the organism's nervous system without distortion or hindrance.

Such a person knows everything about his or her nature; no aspect of the personality is closed off. It follows that the personality is flexible, not only receptive to the experiences life offers but able to use them in opening up new avenues of perception and expression. In contrast, the personality of the defensive person, operating under conditions of worth, is static, hidden behind roles, unable to assimilate or even to recognize certain experiences.

The fully functioning person can be described as more "emotional" in that he or she experiences a wide range of positive and negative emotions (both joy and sadness, for example) and experiences them more intensely than the defensive person.

2.   Existential Living

The fully functioning person lives fully in every moment of existence. Each experience is perceived as fresh and new, as having never before existed in precisely the same manner. Consequently, there is excitement as each experience unfolds.

Since the healthy person is open to all experience, the self or personality is constantly influenced or refreshed by each experience. The defensive person, however, must distort a new experience to make it congruent with the self; he or she has a preconceived self-structure into which all experiences must fit. The fully functioning person, with no preconceived or rigid self, does not have to control and manipulate experiences and so can participate freely in them.

Obviously, the fully functioning person is adaptable because the self-structure is constantly open to new experiences. There is no rigidity or predictability in such a personality. The person says, in effect, "What I will be in the next moment, and what I will do, grows out of that moment, and cannot be predicted in advance either by me or by others."[6]

Rogers believes that this quality of existential living is the most essential aspect of the healthy personality. The personality is open to everything that happens at the moment and it finds in each experience a structure that can change easily in response to the next moment's experience.

3.   A Trust in One's Own Organism

This principle may best be understood by referring to Rogers' own experience. He wrote: "When an activity feels as though it is valuable or worth doing, it is worth doing. Put another way, I have learned that my total organismic sensing of a situation is more trustworthy than my intellect."[7]

In other words, behaving in a way that feels right is the most reliable guide to deciding on a course of action, more reliable than rational or intellectual factors. The fully functioning person is able to act on momentary and intuitive impulses. There is a great deal of spontaneity and freedom in such behavior but it is not the same as acting rashly or with total disregard for the consequences.

6.   Ibid., p. 188.
7.   Ibid., p. 22.

Because the healthy person is fully open to experience, he or she has access to all information available in a decision-making situation. This information includes the person's needs, relevant social demands, memories of similar past situations, and perception of the current situation. The healthy individual is able—by virtue of being open to all experiences and living them fully—to permit the total organism to consider each aspect of a situation. All relevant factors are weighed and balanced and a decision is reached which will best satisfy all aspects of the situation.

Rogers compares the healthy personality to an electronic computer into which all relevant data have been programmed. The computer considers all aspects of the problem, all options and ramifications, and quickly determines a course of action.

A person who operates solely on a rational or intellectual basis is, in a sense, handicapped, since emotional factors are ignored in the process of reaching a decision. All facets of the organism—conscious, unconscious, emotional, as well as intellectual—must be analyzed in terms of the problem at hand. Since the data used to reach a decision are accurate (not distorted), and since the total personality is participating in the decision-making process, healthy persons come to trust their decisions as they trust themselves.

The defensive person, on the other hand, makes decisions in terms of the proscriptions which guide his or her behavior. For example, he or she may be guided by fear of what other people will think, of violating a rule of etiquette, or of appearing to be foolish. Since the defensive person does not experience fully, he or she does not have complete and accurate data on all aspects of a situation. Rogers compares this person to a computer programmed to use only a portion of the relevant data.

4. A Sense of Freedom

This characteristic of the healthy personality is implicit in our discussion above. Rogers believes that the more psychologically healthy a person is, the more he or she experiences freedom of choice and of action. The healthy person is able to choose freely, with an absence of constraints or inhibitions, between alternative courses of thought and action. In addition, the fully functioning person enjoys a sense of personal power about life and believes that the future is dependent upon himself or herself, not directed by whim, circumstance, or past events. Because of this feeling of freedom and power, the healthy person sees a great many options in life and feels capable of doing anything he or she might want to do.

The defensive person enjoys no such feelings of freedom. This person may choose to behave in a certain way but is unable to translate that free choice into actual behavior. Behavior is determined by factors beyond the person's control, including his or her own defensiveness and the inability to experience all the data needed for decision making. Such a person will have no sense of power over life and no feeling of limitless possibilities. Options are circumscribed and the vision of the future is narrow.

5.   Creativity

All fully functioning persons are highly creative. In view of their other characteristics, it is difficult to see how they could not be. Those who are fully open to all experiences, who trust their own organism, and who are flexible in their decisions and actions are persons who, Rogers notes, will express themselves in creative products and creative living in all spheres of their existence. In addition, they are spontaneous in their behavior, changing, growing, and developing in response to the rich stimuli of life around them.

Creative, spontaneous persons are not noted for conformity or for passive adjustment to social and cultural constraints. Since they lack defensiveness, they are not concerned about possible approbation from others for their behavior. However, they can and often do conform to the requirements of a particular situation if such conformity will help satisfy their needs and enable them to develop their selves to the fullest.

The defensive person, lacking feelings of freedom, closed off from many experiences, and living within predetermined guidelines, is neither creative nor spontaneous. This person is more oriented toward making life safe and predictable, and keeping tensions at a minimum, than in seeking new challenges, stimulation, and excitement. This rigid life style does not provide a nutritious soil for the nourishment of creativity.

Rogers believes that fully functioning persons are more capable of adapting to and surviving drastic changes in environmental conditions. They possess the creativity and spontaneity to cope with even traumatic changes, such as in combat or natural disasters. Thus, Rogers considers fully functioning persons to be a "fit vanguard" in the process of human evolution.

A Personal Comment

There is an appealing simplicity in Rogers' description of the healthy personality, as there was with Allport's criteria. But I think there is a special appeal in Rogers' views that has helped make them so popular—his call to be "me" and to be "now." There seems to be a self-indulgent quality in this, certainly an attraction in an age which stresses the virtue of expressing one's self fully and openly, free of inhibitions and constraints.

My overall reaction to Rogers' position is ambivalent. I find many appealing points but I find discomforting characteristics as well.

It is difficult to disagree with the proposition that healthy persons are capable of self-directed change and growth, of guiding their lives unimpeded by childhood events. This notion is shared by other theorists in this book. Another idea proposed by Rogers and others is the existence of an inherited tendency for psychological growth and actualization, a built-in motivation for psychological health that propels us forward.

Rogers presents unique and intriguing prescriptions for psychological health which I find attractive. The development of the self and the specific ways in which self-concept is influenced by the mother seem to enjoy both empirical and commonsense validation. The importance of positive regard and conditions of worth are also highly persuasive.

Equally refreshing is Rogers' description of psychologically healthy persons as fully open to all experiences. This image offers a zestful and exciting life style. Certainly it is appealing to feel oneself capable of experiencing every sensation and emotion—positive or negative—without feeling threatened.

Fully functioning persons seem fully alive in their capacity to experience deeply the full gamut of emotions, happiness as well as sadness, elation as well as despair. They are intensely feeling individuals. The capacity of the fully functioning person to respond to every moment of experience as fresh and new, to live fully in each moment of existence is exciting to me. To be able to choose and act freely without constraints, to feel a sense of power over life, and to be creative and spontaneous, certainly seem to be hallmarks of a healthy existence.

However, despite the excitement, richness, and diversity inherent in Rogers' description of the healthy personality, several points seem to me to be the antithesis of psychological health and maturity.

Rogers' overall view seems to lack (1) a sense of responsibility to others and (2) clear-cut goals and purposes. The theory appears to invite the individual to exist in a state of total selfishness and self-indulgence. The emphasis is on experiencing, feeling, and living fully for oneself without a corresponding emphasis on love, dedication, or commitment to a cause, purpose, or person other than "me" and "my" fresh experience of each moment. This vision of the healthy personality lacks a sense of an active, caring, responsible relationship to other persons or to society. The fully functioning person seems to be the center of the world, not an interacting, responsible participant in it. The concern is solely with one's own existence, not with fostering the growth and development of another.

I am also troubled by what appears to be an anti-intellectual bias pervading Rogers' position. Decisions are made in terms of whether they feel right, not in terms of logical validity or correctness. While Rogers does not deny the usefulness of reason and logic, these factors seem to be secondary to a person's emotional feelings about a situation or decision.

Rogers' notion that one's perception of the world is to be taken as the only reality is also disturbing.[8] What troubles me is not the idea that we perceive the world subjectively (for there is little question that we do), but rather the explicit suggestion that this is a necessary component of psychological health. Should we not strive to know ourselves and our world as objectively as is humanly possible? Can we respond realistically to the world around us if we do not know that world in objective terms?

Perceiving and responding to the environment solely in terms of the images we form of it seems tantamount to living in a fantasy world of our own construction. The idea that mental illness is characterized by such a splitting off from reality is an old one. Indeed, insanity is usually defined as a condition in which contact with reality has been lost. It is difficult to reconcile this point with Rogers' idea that one's subjective perception of reality *is* reality, and that this is a characteristic of psychological health. However, there is no denying the value of this proposition for Rogers' own life. He has effectively practiced what he preaches and it obviously works for him. Thus, the concept has been validated in the laboratory of his own existence.

Leaving aside my difficulties with these aspects of Rogers' position, it must be noted that his theory, as reflected in client-centered therapy and in his recent work with encounter groups and sensitivity sessions, has been immensely popular. It seems, therefore, to be filling

8. The idea that our perception is subjective is an old one. The British philosopher George Berkely said much the same thing in the eighteenth century and contemporary research in psychology has confirmed it.

a need of large numbers of people. His therapeutic endeavors have been successful in changing personalities from defensive postures to more open, freely experiencing, spontaneous ones. His case reports present (often in the client's words) inspirational accounts of enhanced and enriched personalities who have become self-confident, spontaneous, and creative in meeting life's demands.

It is difficult to argue with the general proposition that it is healthier to be open to experience, to live fully and appreciate every moment of life, to be flexible and not afraid of all aspects of human existence. Clearly it is more desirable to feel free, to have confidence in one's abilities, and to feel a sense of power in shaping one's life. Such characteristics certainly speak of psychological health rather than neurosis. Such persons would indeed seem to be functioning intensely and vitally. Whether they are functioning at the highest level of human potential, however, remains to be seen.

BIBLIOGRAPHY

Rogers, C. R. *Client-Centered Therapy: Its Current Practice, Implications, and Theory.* Boston: Houghton Mifflin, 1951.

———. *On Becoming a Person: A Therapist's View of Psychotherapy.* Boston: Houghton Mifflin, 1961.

———. Toward a science of the person. *Journal of Humanistic Psychology,* 1963, *3*, 72–92.

———. Actualizing tendency in relation to motives and to consciousness. In M. R. Jones, ed., *Nebraska Symposium on Motivation, 1963.* Lincoln: University of Nebraska Press, 1963.

———. Autobiography. In E. G. Boring and G. Lindzey, eds., *History of Psychology in Autobiography,* Vol. 5. New York: Appleton-Century-Crofts, 1967.

Hall, M. H. A conversation with Carl Rogers. *Psychology Today,* 1967, *1*, 18–21, 62–66.

4

The productive person
Fromm's model

When Erich Fromm (1900–) was twelve years old, a lovely and talented young woman, a friend of his family, committed suicide. Fromm was greatly shocked by this tragedy for which there seemed to be no plausible explanation. No one could understand why she had chosen to end her life. The event touched Fromm deeply but it was not his first encounter with irrational behavior, nor would it be his last.

As the only child of neurotic parents, Fromm grew up in a household he described as tense. His father was moody, anxious, and morose; his mother was prone to bouts of intense depression. It seems that young Fromm was not surrounded by healthy personalities. His boyhood and adolescence provided a living laboratory for the observation of neurotic behavior.

At age fourteen, Fromm saw irrationality engulf his German homeland when World War I erupted. He was astonished by the hatred that swept the country. He watched with dismay as propaganda whipped the German people into an orgy of hysterical fanaticism. Friends and acquaintances were affected; a much-admired teacher became a bloodlusting fanatic; and many relatives and older friends died in the trenches. These events disturbed Fromm immensely. He began to wonder "why decent and reasonable people suddenly all go crazy."[1]

Out of these confusing experiences Fromm developed the desire to understand the nature and source of irrational human behavior. More than anything else, the impact of World War I on the German people provided for him a direction in which to seek the answer. He began to suspect that it was the impact of large-scale socioeconomic,

1. R. I. Evans, *Dialogue with Erich Fromm* (New York: Harper & Row, 1966), p. 57.

political, and historical forces that influenced the nature of human personality.

Fromm pursued this idea at the University of Heidelberg, where he studied psychology, philosophy, and sociology. He studied the works of leading economic, social, and political theorists, particularly Karl Marx, Max Weber, and Herbert Spencer. After receiving his Ph.D. in 1922, he underwent psychoanalytic training in orthodox Freudian analysis in Munich and Berlin. For a time he thought he had found the answer to human irrationality in the works of Freud, but this did not satisfy him for long.

In the years that followed, Fromm developed and refined his own theory of personality in a series of highly popular books. His system depicts personality as determined by the social forces that affect the individual in childhood as well as by the historical forces that have influenced the development of the human species.

"We are what we have to be," Fromm wrote, "in accordance with the necessities of the society in which we live."[2] Since social and cultural forces are so important, Fromm believes that it is necessary to analyze the structure of society (past and present) in order to understand the structure of the individual members of that society. Thus, the nature of society is the key to understanding and changing human personality. As is the culture, so shall be the individual. Whether a personality is healthy or unhealthy depends on the culture, which fosters or thwarts positive human growth and development.

FROMM'S APPROACH TO PERSONALITY

Fromm views personality as very much a product of culture. As such, he believes that mental health must be defined in terms of how well society adjusts to the basic needs of all individuals, not in terms of how well individuals adjust to society. Therefore, psychological health is not so much an individual affair as a social one. The key factor is how sufficiently a society satisfies human needs.

An unhealthy or sick society creates in its members hostility, suspicion, and distrust, and inhibits the full growth of the individual selves. A healthy society allows its members to develop love for one another, to be productive and creative, to sharpen and refine their powers of reason and objectivity, and it facilitates the emergence of fully functioning selves.

Fromm believes that all of us possess an inherent striving for

2. Ibid., p. 9.

emotional health and well-being, an innate tendency for productive living, for harmony and love. Given the opportunity, this inherited tendency will blossom, allowing us to develop to the fullest utilization of our potential. But when social forces interfere with the natural tendency for growth, the result is irrational and neurotic behavior; sick societies produce sick people.

The dependence of mental health on the nature of society means that each society sets forth its own definition of mental health, and this definition may vary with different times and places. For example, in the nineteenth and early twentieth centuries it was considered proper, or sane, behavior to save and hoard. Persons who spent money they did not have (akin to buying on credit) deviated from the norm and were thought to be behaving irrationally. In recent times, however, the economic structure has depended on continuing consumption, and buying on credit is desirable—even necessary—if the economy is to expand. The person who buys only what he or she can pay cash for is considered out of step with the times and less than psychologically healthy. Thus, in the space of one or two generations, the definition of healthy and unhealthy behavior with regard to spending habits has been reversed.

Fromm's intensive investigation of the history of the human species yields examples of many behaviors prescribed as healthy in one culture or era and unhealthy in another.

As an outgrowth of his historical analyses, Fromm describes the essence of the human condition as *loneliness and insignificance*. (This position is not as pessimistic as it might seem at first glance.) He speaks of existential and historical divisions in human nature which result from our evolution from the lower animals, a process that allowed us to achieve considerable freedom, but at the expense of security and belongingness.

We are unique and lonely creatures, according to Fromm. As a result of our evolution from lower animals we are no longer at one with nature; we have transcended nature. Unlike animal behavior, our behavior is not tied to instinctive mechanisms. However, the most important difference between humans and the lower animals lies in our powers of self-awareness, reason, and imagination. Human beings *know;* we know that we are ultimately powerless, that we will die, and that we are separate from other animals and from nature.

Thus, our reason and imagination are both a curse and a blessing. Knowledge and awareness mean greater freedom than lower animals have, but they also mean alienation from the rest of nature. Human beings are "homeless"; the more freedom we have acquired through the ages, the more insecurity we have developed.

Fromm believes that this split between freedom and security is repeated in the history of the human species as well as in the development of each human being. In every succeeding period of history, as humans have gained increasing relief from rigid social and religious constraints, the gap between freedom and security has grown wider. The greatest gap has occurred since the end of the Middle Ages to the present day.

What was the human situation during the Middle Ages? There was virtually no individual freedom. The feudal system and the Catholic Church rigidly defined each person's place in society. A person could not leave the role or the geographic location into which he or she had been born. The culture dictated where a person lived, his or her work, style of dress, and acceptable modes of behavior.

This is far from the condition of individual freedom we know in American culture today. Yet Fromm believes there was a compensation for this lack of freedom in the Middle Ages—people felt secure in their roles in society. One had no doubt about who and what one was. Therefore, one felt stable and had a sense of belongingness.

What has happened since then? The Middle Ages were followed by the social upheavals of the Renaissance and the Protestant Reformation, which greatly expanded personal freedom but, Fromm argues, with a consequent decline in security. There was greater freedom in interactions with other people and with God, and societal roles were more flexible. There was more power and choice over personal lives. Of course, we achieved this greater sense of freedom at the expense of the ties that had provided security and a sense of belonging. As a result, the human condition became characterized by feelings of isolation and alienation, not only from nature but from society and our fellow humans as well. We are free from slavery and a rigid social order, but because of our increased insecurity we are not free to develop our full potentialities, the full essence of our selves.

The basic problem which confronts all of us is to find a resolution for the dichotomies in our existence and to find new forms of union with nature, with others, and with ourselves. All human existence is determined by this inescapable choice between "regression and progression, between return to animal existence and arrival at human existence."[3] Our passions and needs are oriented toward finding a solution to this fundamental problem.

---

3. E. Fromm, *The Sane Society* (New York: Holt, Rinehart & Winston, 1955), pp. 27–28.

THE MOTIVATION OF THE HEALTHY PERSONALITY

As living organisms, we are motivated to satisfy the basic physiological needs of hunger, thirst, and sex which motivate all animals. Aside from our greater flexibility in satisfying these needs, they do not differ between ourselves and lower animals and they are of minimal importance in influencing human personality.

What is important in influencing personality are the psychological needs which lower animals do not possess. All human beings—healthy and unhealthy—are motivated by these needs; the difference between them is in the way these needs are satisfied. Healthy persons satisfy psychological needs in creative, productive ways. Unhealthy persons satisfy them in irrational ways.

Fromm proposed five needs which derive from the freedom-security dichotomy.

1.   Relatedness

Human beings are aware of the loss of their primary ties with nature and with each other. We know that each of us is separate, alone, and powerless. As a result, we must seek new ties with other human beings; we must find a sense of relatedness with them to replace our lost ties with nature. Fromm believes that satisfaction of this need to relate to or unite with others is vital for psychological health. Irrational behavior, even insanity, is the inevitable result of failure to satisfy this need.

There are several ways to find relatedness. Some are destructive (unhealthy) and others constructive (healthy). A person could try to unite with the world by becoming *submissive* to another person, to a group, or to an ideal such as God. By submitting, the person is no longer alone but rather belongs to someone or something bigger than the self. Alternately, a person could try to relate to the world by achieving *power* over it, by forcing others to submit to him or her.

Both of these approaches involve a dependence on others for security. As a result, the person has neither freedom nor self-integrity but lives in and from other people. Therefore, these approaches are doomed because the submissive or the dominating person is not free to develop the full essence of the self, since his or her security depends on those whom they submit to or control.

The healthy way of relating to the world is through *love*. This satisfies the need for security and at the same time allows a sense of integrity and individuality. Fromm does not define love solely in the erotic sense; his definition includes the love of parent for child, love of oneself, and the larger sense of solidarity with and love of all people.

Failure to satisfy the need for relatedness in any manner results in *narcissism,* the essense of irrational behavior. Narcissistic persons have as their only reality their own thoughts, feelings, and needs. Since their entire focus is on themselves, they are unable to relate to the outside world or to other persons; they are unable to experience objectively anything beyond themselves, perceiving everything from their own subjective point of view.[4]

In Fromm's system, persons who cannot perceive the world objectively, who can perceive it only in terms of their inner processes, have withdrawn into themselves and lost all contact with reality. This is the traditional definition of insanity.

2. Transcendence

Closely allied with the need for relatedness is the human need to rise above or transcend our passive roles as creatures. Aware of the accidental nature of birth and death, of the random character of existence, human beings are driven to transcend the state of having been created to become instead *creators,* active shapers of their own lives. Fromm believes that in the act of creating (children, ideas, art, or material goods) human beings rise above the passive and accidental nature of existence, thereby achieving a sense of purpose and freedom.

Creating is the ideal or healthy means of transcending the passive animal state which human beings cannot accept because of their powers of reason and imagination. But what happens if a person is unable to be creative? The need for transcendence must be satisfied, if not in a healthy way, then in an unhealthy way.

Fromm believes that the alternative to creativeness is *destructiveness.* "If I cannot create life," he wrote, "I can destroy it. To destroy life makes me also transcend it."[5] In acts of destruction, a person is able to rise above the passive state. Destructiveness, like creativeness, is an active involvement with the world. These are the only choices a person has, to create or destroy, love or hate; there are no other ways of achieving transcendence.

Destructiveness and creativeness are both deeply rooted in

4. This subjectivity, in contrast, is the essence of Rogers' position as to what constitutes mental health.
5. E. Fromm, *The Sane Society* (New York: Holt, Rinehart & Winston, 1955), p. 37.

human nature. Creativity, however, is the primary potential and it leads to psychological health. Destructiveness leads only to the suffering of the object of destruction and of the destroyer as well.

3. Rootedness

The essence of the human condition—loneliness and insignificance—arises from the severance of the primary ties with nature. Without these roots the person is helpless, clearly an intolerable condition. New roots must be established to replace the former ties with nature. As with the other needs, rootedness can be achieved in a positive or a negative way.

The ideal way is to establish a feeling of *brotherliness* with fellow human beings, a sense of involvement, love, concern, and participation in society. This sense of solidarity with others satisfies the need for rootedness, for connection, and for relatedness with the world.

The unhealthy way to achieve rootedness is through the maintenance of the childhood *incestuous ties* with the mother. In a sense, such a person is never able to leave home and continues to cling to the security of these early maternal ties. Incestuous ties can extend beyond the infant-mother relationship to include the whole family cluster and, in a larger sense, the community.

In a still larger sense, the person could maintain incestuous ties with the country. "Nationalism is our form of incest, is our idolatry, is our insanity. 'Patriotism' is its cult."[6] This attitude places country above the interests of humanity at large. A love focused on one's country, Fromm argues, excludes love for the people of other countries and is thus a form of idolatrous worship, not love.

By maintaining incestuous ties at any level, a person closes off certain experiences and restricts love and solidarity to only some human beings. This situation does not allow full caring, sharing, and participation with the world at large which is a requisite for psychological health. A person who loves only some human beings, who feels a sense of brotherliness with a limited portion of humanity, is unable to develop all of his or her human potential.

4. A Sense of Identity

Human beings also need a sense of identity as unique individuals, an identity which places them apart from others in terms of their feelings about who and what they are.

6.   Ibid., p. 58

The healthy way of satisfying this need is *individuality*, the process by which a person achieves a definite sense of self-identity. The extent to which we each experience a unique sense of selfhood depends on how successful we are in breaking the incestuous ties with our family, clan, or nation. Persons with well-developed feelings of individuality experience themselves as more in control of their own lives, instead of having their lives shaped by others.

The unhealthy way of forming a sense of identity is by *conforming* to the characteristics of a nation, race, religion, or occupation. In this way identity is defined in reference to the qualities of a group, not in reference to the qualities of the self. By adhering to the norms, values, and behaviors of such groups, a person does find a kind of identity; however, it is at the expense of the self. In this case, the self is borrowed from the group and does not provide a unique sense of individuality. The conforming self is not genuine, it does not belong exclusively to the individual, and the person will be unable to achieve full humanness.

5. A Frame of Orientation

Related to the search for a unique sense of self is the search for a frame of reference or context within which to interpret all the phenomena of the world. Each individual must formulate a consistent image of the world which allows for the understanding of all events and experiences.

The ideal basis for the frame of orientation is through *reason*, by means of which a person develops a realistic and objective picture of the world. Implicit in this is the capacity to see the world (including the self) in objective terms, to reflect the world accurately and not distort it through the subjective lenses of one's own needs and fears.

Fromm places great importance on the objective perception of reality. The more objective our perception, the more we are in touch with reality; thus, the more mature and better equipped we are to cope with the world. Reason must be developed and applied to all aspects of life. If, for example, a person is ruled by myth or superstition in one facet of life, then the applicability of reason to other facets of life will be inhibited. Fromm likens reason to love; neither can function fully if restricted to a single object.

A less desirable way of constructing a frame of orientation is through *irrationality*. This involves a subjective view of the world; events and experiences are seen not as they really are but as the person wishes them to be. Of course, even a subjective framework does provide a picture of the world. Although it may be illusory, it is still real to the individual who holds it. Unfortunately, this kind of orientation removes the person from contact with reality.

Psychologist Salvatore Maddi notes similarities between some of Fromm's needs and Allport's propriate functions.[7] Parallels are drawn between the need for transcendence and propriate striving, the need for rootedness and self-extension, the need for identity and self-identity and self-esteem, and the need for a frame of orientation and rational coping.

We have discussed the healthy and unhealthy ways of satisfying the five needs in Fromm's theory. This has already given us some idea of the nature of the healthy personality.

THE NATURE OF THE HEALTHY PERSONALITY

Fromm provides a clearly drawn portrait of the healthy personality. Such a person loves fully, is creative, has highly developed powers of reason, perceives the world and the self objectively, possesses a firm sense of identity, is related to and rooted in the world, is the subject or agent of self and destiny, and is free of incestuous ties.

Fromm calls the healthy personality the *productive orientation,* a concept similar to Allport's mature personality and Maslow's self-actualizing person.[8] It represents the fullest utilization or realization of human potential. By using the word "orientation," Fromm makes the point that it is a general attitude or viewpoint which encompasses all aspects of life, the intellectual, emotional, and sensory responses to people, objects, and events in the world as well as to the self.

Being productive means using all of one's powers and potentialities. The word "productive" may be misleading, for we tend to think of it in terms of producing something such as material goods, works of art, or ideas. Fromm means much more than this. It might be useful to think of productivity as synonymous with full functioning, self-actualizing, loving, openness, and experiencing.

However, there is one sense in which the healthy, productive personality does produce something and it is the person's most im-

7. S. R. Maddi, *Personality Theories: A Comparative Analysis,* 3rd ed. (Homewood, Ill.: Dorsey Press, 1976), p. 123.
8. See Chapter 2 (pp. 6–23) and Chapter 5 (pp. 58–81).

portant product: the self. Healthy persons create their selves by giving birth to all their potentialities, by becoming all they are capable of
becoming, by fulfilling all their capacities.

Four additional facets of the healthy personality may help clarify
what Fromm means by the productive orientation. These are productive love, productive thinking, happiness, and conscience.

Productive love involves a free and equal human relationship in
which the partners are able to maintain their individuality. One's self
is not absorbed or lost in the love of another person. Rather than being diminished in productive love, the self is expanded, allowed to
fully unfold. A feeling of relatedness is achieved, but one's identity
and independence are maintained.

The attainment of productive love is one of life's more difficult
achievements. We do not "fall" in love; we must expend a great deal
of effort because productive love involves four challenging characteristics—care, responsibility, respect, and knowledge. Loving others
means caring (in the sense of taking care of them), being vitally
concerned with their well-being, and fostering their growth and
development. This implies taking responsibility for others in the
sense of wanting to be responsive to their needs. Also, loved ones are
looked upon with respect and acceptance of their individuality; they
are loved for who and what they are. And in order to respect them we
must have full knowledge of them; we must understand objectively
who and what they are.

You can see why productive love is difficult to achieve. It is an
activity rather than a passion. Productive love is not restricted to
erotic love but may be brotherly love (the love of all human beings) or
maternal love (the love of mother for child).

Productive thinking involves intelligence, reason, and objectivity.
The productive thinker is motivated by a strong interest in the object
of thought. He or she is affected by it and concerned with it. There is
an intimate relationship between the object of thought and the
thinker in which the person can examine the object in an objective,
respectful, and caring manner. Productive thinking focuses on the
whole of the phenomenon under study rather than on isolated bits
and pieces of it. Fromm believes that all great discoveries and insights
involve productive thinking in that the thinkers are motivated by care,
respect, and concern to objectively evaluate the totality of the
problem.

Happiness is an integral part and outcome of living in accordance
with the productive orientation; it accompanies all productive activity.
Happiness is not merely a pleasant feeling or state but rather a condi-

tion which enhances the total organism, bringing about increased vitality, physical health, and fulfillment of one's potentialities. Productive people are happy people. A feeling of happiness, Fromm wrote, is proof of how successful a person is "in the art of living. Happiness is [our] greatest achievement."[9]

Fromm distinguishes two types of *conscience:* authoritarian and humanistic. The *authoritarian conscience* represents an internalized outside authority which directs the person's behavior. The authority could be parents, the state, or any other group, and it regulates behavior through the person's fear of punishment for violating the authority's moral code. If the person behaves contrary to that moral code (or even thinks of such behavior), he or she experiences guilt. Thus, the arbiter of behavior and thought is external to the self and acts to inhibit the self's full functioning and growth. The authoritarian conscience is antithetical to productive living.

The *humanistic conscience* is the voice of the self and not of some external agent. The healthy personality's guide for behavior is internal and individual. The person behaves in accordance with what is appropriate for the full functioning and total unfolding of the personality, behaviors which produce a feeling of internal approval and happiness. The person is saying, in effect, "I will do this because I owe it to myself," not "I must do this because my parents or the culture demand it of me." Thus, the productive, healthy personality is self-directed and self-regulated.

The productive orientation is an ideal state or goal of human development and it has not yet been achieved in any society. As we discussed, mental health, in Fromm's view, is defined with reference to society, for the nature of the social structure fosters or inhibits psychological health. If sick societies produce sick people, then the only way to attain the productive orientation is by living in a sane, healthy society, one which promotes productiveness.

Fromm envisions this society—*humanistic communitarian socialism*—as one in which no person is exploited or manipulated for a purpose other than the achievement of maximum development of the self. In this future society, our humanness will be the focus; economic and political maneuvers will have as their aim the fostering of human growth and full functioning. The ideals of this society are love, human solidarity, and brotherhood, the responsible participation of each individual in his or her own life and in society, the direction of

9. E. Fromm, *Man for Himself* (New York: Holt, Rinehart & Winston, 1947), p. 191.

behavior by each person's sense of self, and the full, productive use of every human being.

Obviously, we do not live in such a sane society. (And if history is any indication, we may never do so.) However, the fact that our society is not perfect does not mean that we cannot attain a degree of psychological health. Fromm believes that it is impossible to reach full productivity in our present social structure but that it is possible to achieve partial productivity.

To understand how this is brought about, we must discuss Fromm's alternatives to the productive orientation, the *nonproductive orientations:* receptive, exploitative, hoarding, and marketing. Like the productive orientation, these are essentially character traits, ways in which persons orient themselves to the world around them. The personality of any individual is a blend of some or all of these traits; no one is exclusively one type, although one orientation is usually more dominant than the others. We shall examine these less-than-healthy orientations and see how they can be partially transformed by the productive orientation in order for a person to achieve an approximation of a fully productive personality.

Persons with the *receptive orientation* are passive receivers in their relations with others. They are not capable of producing, creating, or giving love. They depend entirely on external sources—spouse, friends, or society—for everything they need. Since they are so dependent and can do nothing for themselves, they can be paralyzed with anxiety and fright when left alone.

The society which fosters the development of this orientation officially sanctions and encourages the exploitation and manipulation of one group of people by another. An obvious example is a slave culture in which the slaves can only act receptively and passively toward their masters. Although this does not represent contemporary American society, Fromm believes that examples of this kind of orientation still exist.

The *exploitative orientation* also characterizes persons who are directed by external sources. However, instead of expecting to receive from others, they are driven to take from them by force or guile or whatever method is successful. Again, these persons are incapable of producing or creating by themselves and so they get love, possessions, even thoughts and emotions, only by appropriating them from others. This orientation is characteristic of a totalitarian or fascist society, a setting in which strong, domineering leaders rule by force. This orientation can occur in any kind of society, however.

Persons with the *hoarding orientation* do not expect anything from outside sources, neither by receiving nor taking. These persons achieve security by saving and hoarding—material possessions, thoughts, or emotions. Hoarding personalities seem to build walls around themselves so as not to let their possessions out (and not to let anything in). All aspects of these persons become private possessions and must not be shared with or given to others. Societies which foster the Puritan ethic of thrift and where hard work and saving are virtues promote this orientation.

The *marketing orientation* is the primary character trait in capitalistic societies such as the United States. The personality or self is valued only as a commodity to be sold or exchanged in return for success. Our sense of esteem, worth, and pride depends on how successful we are in selling ourselves. Success or failure depends not on developing productive capacities to the fullest, nor on integrity, knowledge, or skills, but rather on how well we project our personality to others. Superficial qualities—smiling, being agreeable, knowing the right people, laughing at the boss's jokes—are more important than inner qualities.

Fromm has also introduced a fifth pair of nonproductive orientations: necrophilious-biophilious. The *necrophilious orientation* describes a person obsessed with sickness and death. *Biophilious,* a more productive orientation, describes a person who fights against death and decay and who is concerned with the growth and development of the self.

These nonproductive orientations appear to be unhealthy ways of relating to the world. However, Fromm points out that each of these orientations has desirable and undesirable aspects. Each orientation encompasses a continuum, or range, of behavior from completely unproductive to at least moderately productive. For example, in the receptive orientation the behavioral trait "submissive" (an unproductive way of behaving) can be transformed into the trait "devotion" (a more productive characteristic). The unprincipled trait can be transformed into adaptable behavior, the cowardly trait into sensitive behavior, and the spineless trait into the polite.

Fromm considers the undesirable side of the nonproductive orientations to be distortions of normal character traits which are necessary for survival. We all must, on occasion, be able to receive things from others, or take them, or save or exchange. We must at times obey authority, lead others, be alone, or be aggressive. Only if our orientation is totally unproductive does the occasional need to accept, take, save, or exchange turn into the compulsion to receive, exploit, hoard, or market. Again, the key to psychological health is the strength of the productive tendencies.

Unfortunately, Fromm does not tell us how this transformation from unproductive to productive takes place. In general, it has to do with the strength of the productive orientation. The greater its strength, the more successful it will be in transforming undesirable facets of the nonproductive orientations to more desirable ones. The more of these undesirable behaviors that are changed, the healthier will be the personality.

Positive and negative aspects of the nonproductive orientations are listed below. You can see how the positive aspects are characteristic of psychological health and the negative aspects characteristic of psychological ill health.

Positive and Negative Aspects of Nonproductive Orientations[10]

RECEPTIVE ORIENTATION (ACCEPTING)

Positive Aspect	*Negative Aspect*
Accepting	Passive, without initiative
Responsive	Opinionless, characterless
Devoted	Submissive
Modest	Without pride
Charming	Parasitical
Adaptable	Unprincipled
Socially adjusted	Servile, without self-confidence
Idealistic	Unrealistic
Sensitive	Cowardly
Polite	Spineless
Optimistic	Wishful thinking
Trusting	Gullible
Tender	Sentimental

EXPLOITATIVE ORIENTATION (TAKING)

Active	Exploitative
Able to take initiative	Aggressive
Able to make claims	Egocentric
Proud	Conceited
Impulsive	Rash
Self-confident	Arrogant
Captivating	Seducing

HOARDING ORIENTATION (PRESERVING)

Practical	Unimaginative
Economical	Stingy
Careful	Suspicious
Reserved	Cold
Patient	Lethargic
Cautious	Anxious

---

10. Ibid., pp. 114–16.

HOARDING ORIENTATION (PRESERVING) (Cont.)

Positive Aspect	Negative Aspect
Steadfast, tenacious	Stubborn
Imperturbable	Indolent
Composed under stress	Inert
Orderly	Pedantic
Methodical	Obsessional
Loyal	Possessive

MARKETING ORIENTATION (EXCHANGING)

Purposeful	Opportunistic
Able to change	Inconsistent
Youthful	Childish
Forward-looking	Without a future or a past
Open-minded	Without principle and values
Social	Unable to be alone
Experimenting	Aimless
Undogmatic	Relativistic
Efficient	Overactive
Curious	Tactless
Intelligent	Intellectualistic
Adaptable	Undiscriminating
Tolerant	Indifferent
Witty	Silly
Generous	Wasteful

These positive and negative aspects of the nonproductive orientations are really opposite sides of the same coin, the same behaviors displayed in constructive or destructive ways. These pairs of behaviors do not represent either/or situations; each exists on a continuum with many shades of difference between the two extremes.

A final question must be asked about Fromm's version of the healthy personality: how does one become a fully productive person? What determines if a person's character will be predominantly productive or nonproductive, healthy or sick? We noted that the history of the development of the human species is recreated in the development of each person. As the growing child becomes increasingly independent of the mother, he or she becomes less secure. Caught in a vise between security and freedom, the child deals with the growing freedom by means of one of three escape mechanisms, depending upon the parents' behavior toward the child. (Note that the parents' behavior toward the child is determined, in large measure, by the nature of the society.) These escape mechanisms are symbiotic relatedness, withdrawal-destructiveness, and love.

In *symbiotic relatedness* the child remains dependent on others and never achieves a state of independence and freedom. In a very real sense such a person escapes the insecurity of freedom by becoming a part of someone else. This behavior is manifested in either masochistic or sadistic ways, by submitting to others or having power over them. The *withdrawal-destructiveness* mechanism of escape involves either withdrawing from others or trying to destroy them. Both behaviors involve maintaining a separation from others, thus avoiding a situation of dependency. *Love,* the most ideal form of escape, is the basis for the development of the productive orientation.

Fromm did not elaborate on the specific parental behaviors responsible for the emergence of these escape mechanisms. However, he clearly points out the importance to psychological health of the way in which the parents treat the child, particularly during the first five years of life. It is certainly desirable to have productive, healthy parents (as most of our other theorists note as well).

A PERSONAL COMMENT

Fromm's interpretation of the origin of the healthy personality stresses the impact of social, economic, and political forces on the individual. More than any other theorist he has focused on our life history as individuals and as a species and on the kind of society in which we live.

I believe that both the reading of history and our personal experiences serve to support Fromm's emphasis on the role of social forces in shaping personality. For example, we can readily see differences in basic values, needs, and fears (orientations) between persons raised during the severe depression of the 1930s and those raised during the affluent years of the 1960s. Their outlooks on life are totally different, formed by disparate economic and social conditions.

Yet Fromm tells us (and our own experience and knowledge of history verify) that not everyone is a prisoner of the society in which he or she was raised. Not everyone raised in the 1930s shares the orientation of insecurity with regard to financial matters. Not everyone in Nazi Germany was molded by party propaganda into an anti-Semite or developed an exploitative orientation. Not every slave in nineteenth-century America became receptive in orientation; some led uprisings and others, once freed, developed other orientations.

Thus, it is possible to overcome the effects of culture. If this were not true, there would be no hope for achieving psychological health in our own less-than-ideal society, yet we know that many persons do. Thus, while we are certainly influenced by our culture, we are not irrevocably doomed by it. Every form of society—from feudal to fascist—has produced some examples of psychologically healthy persons, and Fromm is optimistic about the possibility of approximating the productive orientation, even under repressive social orders.

Fromm's position offers hope to all of us. The innate striving for psychological health is very strong. Of course, the psychological forces preventing productivity are also strong—witness the high incidence of emotional disturbance in our time—but health, productivity, and love sometimes prevail against harsh opposition.

I am less in agreement with Fromm's assertion that loneliness and insignificance are the essence of the human condition because we are no longer at one with nature. Do we really long to return to the union with nature that characterized our prehuman past? Are we truly bereft because we have broken free of our dependence on our natural roots? Do we feel more homeless than animals? It is hard for me to answer these questions affirmatively; I suspect the opposite to be true. Is it not possible that human beings are grateful that we have escaped these alleged ties with our animal past, that we have reason and imagination which enable us to dream of and to achieve the distinctly human conditions of existence, and that we can have some measure of control over our own lives? I think Fromm may have admitted to this when he described as one of the basic human needs transcending our roles as passive creatures, rising above our animal state.

However, even if Fromm's thesis is correct, we are still not condemned to perpetual isolation and insignificance. We can at least partially recapture that union by attaining feelings of relatedness, rootedness, love, and brotherhood with our fellow human beings, conditions that seem highly desirable no matter what their motivation might be.

On another issue, it seems to me that Fromm's healthy, productive personality is a less selfish individual than Rogers' fully functioning person. The productive personality is characterized by a responsible interaction with others, and by love, participation, care, respect, and knowledge. The focus is not entirely on self, although the self is best served by positive relations of giving to and loving others. In Fromm's view, we need other persons for our own well-being.

Fromm's productive personality, like Allport's mature personality, is firmly anchored in reality. Healthy persons perceive the world (other persons, events, and their selves) in objective terms, unlike Rogers' fully functioning person. Productive persons do not live in a subjective world of their own construction but are in and of the real world. Also, their frame of reference is based on reason, not emotion. Decisions are taken and choices made not just because they feel right but because they appear to be logically correct and valid.

There is a strong sense of self-identity and self-shaping in Fromm's productive orientation. We actively direct the course of our own lives; we are not satisfied with passivity. We must in some way move to change the world. How much better equipped we are to undertake these important tasks if we have an objective perception of ourselves and of other people, if we respond to the world as it really is.

Another characteristic of Fromm's healthy personality I find appealing is that we strive to develop and fulfill all our capabilities. Healthy, productive persons are strongly and fully in use, stretching, extending, and elaborating their unique qualities. Again we see the sense of being in control and of having power over oneself and one's destiny.

Fromm is the first theorist discussed thus far who equates psychological health with happiness. Happiness is an integral part of the healthy personality, not an accidental by-product (as with Allport and Rogers). Happiness results from productive living and it fosters and promotes even greater levels of productivity. Happiness is so much a part of healthy living that it can be taken as evidence of the degree of psychological health a person has achieved.

I have the impression that Fromm's definition of psychological health is a restatement of basic, age-old themes and prescriptions. As with Allport, there is the sense of timeless truths. Indeed, Fromm admits to this. His concepts, he notes, parallel the teachings of great spiritual leaders of the past. He takes this similarity as further support for the wisdom and validity of his position. He believes that all great religious and philosophical ideals were based on perceptive insights into human nature and the conditions necessary for the fruition of full humanness. The same norms and beliefs have been urged upon us in different places and periods of history and there is no evidence that one influenced another. It seems to Fromm, therefore, that these are basic truths since they recur in the teachings of Moses, Lao-tse, Buddha, Socrates, and Jesus. All preached similar values for the ideal human existence.

Fromm has reiterated these prescriptions within a framework of psychoanalytic observations of individuals and his own interpretation of human history. This may be another case of old wine in yet another new bottle but it is the content, not the container, that is rich in value and long lasting.

BIBLIOGRAPHY

Evans, R. I. *Dialogue with Erich Fromm.* New York: Harper & Row, 1966.

Fromm, E. *Escape from Freedom.* New York: Holt, Rinehart & Winston, 1941.

——. *Man for Himself.* New York: Holt, Rinehart & Winston, 1947.

——. *The Sane Society.* New York: Holt, Rinehart & Winston, 1955.

——. *The Revolution of Hope: Toward a Humanized Technology.* New York: Harper & Row, 1968.

Hausdorff, D. *Erich Fromm.* Boston: Twayne, 1972.

5

The self-actualizing person
Maslow's model

In 1941, a few days after the Japanese attack on Pearl Harbor, Abraham Maslow (1908–1970) was driving home from his teaching job at Brooklyn College when his car was stopped by a parade. It was a pitiful, rag-tag parade composed of an assortment of Boy Scouts and older persons wearing outdated uniforms. The American flag flew at the head of the column and an off-key flute bravely sounded patriotic tunes.

Maslow, an intensely compassionate man, watched the line of bedraggled marchers pass his car and started to cry. "Tears began to run down my face," he wrote. "That moment changed my whole life and determined what I have done since."[1] He resolved to devote his life to an attempt to discover a "psychology for the peace table," a psychology which would deal with the best and the loftiest ideals and potentials of which human beings are capable. He was gripped by a determination that never wavered (even through the poor health that marked his last years) and by a sense of dedication that led him to explore dimensions of the human personality in ways opposed to the psychology establishment and his own past training.

Several earlier experiences also helped to shape Maslow and his study of self-actualization, experiences that were drawn to a specific focus on that December day in 1941. A poor, lonely, unhappy child, he turned, at a very early age, to books and study for solace and they carried him through childhood and adolescence to Cornell and the University of Wisconsin. There, at age twenty, two events broadened

1. M. H. Hall, "Conversation with Abraham H. Maslow," *Psychology Today*, 1968, 2, p. 54.

58

his life considerably: his marriage and his introduction to the be-havioristic psychology of John B. Watson. Maslow said that his life truly began at that point.

At Wisconsin he received solid training in experimental psychology and conducted research with monkeys under the guidance of Harry Harlow. For a time Maslow thought behaviorism would provide answers to all the world's problems, and he applied the behaviorist tools and principles with energy and dedication. But Maslow was a man who was open to all experiences, even ones which contradicted his new-found belief. He began to read Freud and the works of certain philosophers—hardly prescribed reading in the syllabus of behaviorism.

It was a highly personal event, however—the birth of his first child—that finally and completely overthrew his belief in behavior-ism. "The thunderclap that settled things" was how he described the experience. "I'd say that anyone who had a baby couldn't be a be-haviorist."[2] He was awestruck by the mystery of life and by not hav-ing the control over it that behaviorism promised.

In reading Maslow's comments about his life and intellectual development one can almost feel his energy, passion, and basic hu-mility. The experiences that molded him were not abstract theoretical ideas or cold analytical research findings but intensely emotional and personal events. He believed that these experiences strengthened him and he noted three in particular: getting married ("a school in itself"), becoming a father, and his respect and love for his parade of outstanding teachers (Harry Harlow, Erich Fromm, Karen Horney, Ruth Benedict, Max Wertheimer, Alfred Adler).

Indeed, his awe of two of these—Gestalt psychologist Max Wertheimer and anthropologist Ruth Benedict—led to his initial studies of self-actualization and the specific methods by which he studied our lofty potentials. Once again something personal and im-mediate shaped Maslow. His desire to understand these two people occurred at approximately the same time as his encounter with the wartime parade. The latter experience provided him with the com-pelling need to study the best of human nature, to understand the heights which human beings can reach, and Wertheimer and Ben-edict provided him with his first models of just how great those heights could be.

In the years that followed, Maslow recorded his vigorous pursuit of his goal in a number of popular and readable books. Psychologists

2.   Ibid., p. 55.

and nonpsychologists alike have been attracted by Maslow's optimistic and humanistic view of human nature. Many feel that he has provided not only a new dimension to the study of human personality but an entirely new approach to psychology, which one day may be recorded as revolutionary, as were Watson's behaviorism and Freud's psychoanalysis.

Maslow's approach—humanistic, or third force, psychology—is seen by many as a welcome antidote to the mechanistic character of behaviorism and the gloomy, despairing character of psychoanalysis.[3] It is too soon to say how successful this movement will be in changing the nature of psychology, but its followers today are carrying forth the humanistic banner with as much fervor as Maslow first raised it.

Maslow was vitally interested in our potential for growth and toward the end of his life he supported the Esalen Institute in California and other groups involved in the human potential movement. Perhaps it is indicative of the professional support for his work (or at least of the admiration and respect for the man himself) that he was elected president of the American Psychological Association in 1967, three years before his death.

MASLOW'S APPROACH TO PERSONALITY

Maslow's overriding goal was to learn how much potential we have for full human development and expression. He believed that to investigate psychological health, the only kind of person to study was the extremely healthy one. He was critical of Freud and other personality theorists who tried to understand the nature of personality by studying only neurotics and severely disturbed individuals. If we do that, Maslow noted, if we study only the crippled, the immature, and the unhealthy, then we will see only the sick side of human nature, people at their worst rather than at their best. Therefore, Maslow argued, we must study the best, healthiest, and most mature examples of the human species, and he offered the following analogy.

If we want to know how fast human beings can run, we don't study a runner with a broken ankle or a mediocre runner. Instead, we study the Olympic gold medal winner, the best there is. Only in that way can we find out how fast human beings can run. Similarly, only by studying the healthiest personalities can we find out how far we can stretch and develop our capacities.

Maslow had been privileged to know two of the best representa-

---

3. Carl Rogers (Chapter 3, pp. 24–38) is also a pioneer in this movement.

tives of the human species: Max Wertheimer and Ruth Benedict. Wanting very much to understand these exemplary persons, he realized that his training in experimental psychology was inadequate to the task, so he began to observe them in a nonscientific way (he called it "prescientific"). He observed them at every opportunity and gradually reached the conclusion that they possessed certain characteristics which clearly distinguished them from others.

Greatly excited by this finding, Maslow then wanted to know if he could identify other persons who possessed the same characteristics. He scrutinized friends, acquaintances, prominent personalities (both living and deceased), and college students, and selected forty-nine people who appeared to be models of psychological health. He did not release the names of the living subjects but the historical figures include Thomas Jefferson, Abraham Lincoln, Baruch Spinoza, Albert Einstein, Eleanor Roosevelt, J. W. von Goethe, Pablo Casals, John Keats, Adlai Stevenson, Robert Browning, and Martin Buber.

Maslow investigated these individuals using a variety of techniques—interviews, free association, and projective techniques with the living subjects, and analyses of biographical and autobiographical material with the others—and concluded that all human beings are born with *instinctoid needs*. These universal needs motivate us to grow and develop, to actualize ourselves, to become all we are capable of becoming. Thus, the potential for psychological growth and health is present at birth. Whether our potential is fulfilled or actualized depends on the individual and social forces which promote or inhibit self-actualization.

While Maslow recognized that few people in our society achieve self-actualization (less than 1 percent in his view), he nevertheless remained optimistic about the possibility of larger numbers of people reaching this ideal state of full humanness. He stressed that although we can be influenced by unfortunate childhood experiences, we are not immutable victims of these experiences; we can change, grow, and reach high levels of psychological health. In this humanistic view, human beings possess more potential than they realize. Maslow felt that if we could unleash that potential, we could all reach the ideal state of existence that he found in his self-actualizing subjects.

THE MOTIVATION OF THE HEALTHY PERSONALITY

In Maslow's view, all human beings possess an innate striving or tendency to become self-actualizing. There is more to his theory of human motivation, however. We are motivated by other universal and innate needs, arranged in a hierarchy from strongest to weakest. We might think of Maslow's *hierarchy of needs* as a ladder; we must put a foot on the first rung before trying to reach the second, and on the second before the third, and so on. In the same way, the lowest and strongest need must be satisfied before the second-level need emerges, and so on up the hierarchy until the fifth and highest need—self-actualization—appears.

Thus, the prerequisite for achieving self-actualization is satisfying the four needs which stand lower in the hierarchy: (1) the physiological needs, (2) the safety needs, (3) the belonging and love needs, (4) the esteem needs. The needs must be at least partially satisfied in this order before the need for self-actualization appears.

We are not motivated by all five needs at the same time. Only one need is paramount at any given moment; which one depends on which of the other needs have been satisfied. If you have gone several days without food, the physiological need of hunger is dominant. You are not concerned with safety, love, esteem, or self-actualization, but want food more than anything else. Every other human need becomes trivial until you are once again well-fed and no longer uncertain about where the next meal will come from. And, when you are well-fed, hunger as a need no longer exists for you and you become concerned with the safety needs.

Let us examine briefly the five needs in the hierarchy. To reiterate their importance: a person cannot become self-actualizing until each of the lower-level needs has been satisfied to a sufficient degree.

Physiological needs are the obvious ones for food, water, air, sleep, and sex, and their satisfaction is essential for survival. As such, they are the most powerful of all the needs. Beggars on the streets of Indian cities face a daily, life-long battle for sheer survival and thus would never have the opportunity to develop any of the higher needs. In contrast, few persons in our affluent society experience such constant deprivation, and middle-class Americans rarely have to think about satisfaction of survival needs. Since a need gratified is no longer a need, the physiological needs play a minimal role in our lives.

When our physiological needs are taken care of, we are motivated by *safety needs*. These include needs for security, stability, protection, order, and freedom from fear and anxiety. Maslow believed that we all need some degree of routine and predictability. Uncertainty is difficult to tolerate, so we try to achieve as much security, protection, and order as we can. For example, we add to our savings account at the bank, buy insurance, and remain in safe, secure jobs so as not to lose the fringe benefits.

For healthy personalities, the safety needs are not overwhelming or compulsive. We don't save every penny, we take vacations or buy luxury goods instead of additional insurance, and some of us do leave safe jobs for the challenge of new careers. Most of us do not surrender or submit totally to our safety needs, but, at the same time, a complete absence of security and stability causes us discomfort.

When we have achieved a certain level of safety and security we are driven to satisfy the *belonging and love needs.* We may join a group or club, assuming its values and characteristics or wearing its uniform in order to feel a sense of belonging. We satisfy our love needs by establishing an intimate, caring relationship with another person, or with people in general, and in these relationships it is just as important to give love as to receive it.

Maslow believed that it was increasingly difficult to satisfy belonging and love needs in the modern world because of our mobility. We change houses, neighborhoods, cities, even spouses so frequently that we cannot put down roots. We are not in one place long enough to develop a sense of belonging. Many persons today feel lonely and isolated even though they live amidst large numbers of people. We may be surrounded by others on subways, sidewalks, and shopping centers but not have any sense of relationship with them. Indeed, we may not even know those who live next door to us, and we don't make the effort to get to know them because before long we or they will move away.

However, the belonging and love needs must be satisfied and Maslow felt that the difficulty of satisfying them nowadays explains the phenomenal popularity of such group activities as communes, sensitivity groups, and encounter sessions. These are ways of escaping the loneliness and isolation which are the inevitable results of failing to achieve a sense of love and belonging.

If we are fortunate enough to love and to belong, we then need a sense of esteem. Maslow distinguished two types of *esteem needs:* esteem derived from others and self-esteem. Esteem from others is primary; apparently it is difficult for us to think well of ourselves unless we are assured that others think well of us.

Externally derived esteem can be based on reputation, admiration, status, fame, prestige, or social success, all characteristics of how others think of us and react to us. There are many ways of getting others to esteem us: we can display our wealth and importance through the kind of car we drive, the neighborhood we live in, our style of dress, or in admirable and competent behavior.

When we feel a sense of internal or self-esteem, we are confident and secure in ourselves; we feel worthy and adequate. When we lack self-esteem we feel inferior, discouraged, and helpless in dealing with life. In order to have a genuine sense of self-esteem, we must know ourselves well and be able to assess objectively our virtues and weaknesses. We cannot esteem ourselves if we do not know who and what we are.

If we have satisfied all of these needs, we are then driven by the highest need: the *need for self-actualization.* Self-actualization can be defined as the supreme development and use of all our abilities, the fulfillment of all our qualities and capacities. We must become what we have the potential to become. Even though the lower-order needs are satisfied—we feel secure physically and emotionally, have a sense of belonging and love, and feel ourselves to be worthy individuals— we will feel frustrated, restless, and discontent if we fail to attempt to satisfy the need for self-actualization. If that happens we will not be at peace with ourselves and cannot be described as psychologically healthy.

In later writings, Maslow suggested a second hierarchy of needs which operates as an adjunct to the primary hierarchy. The needs in the second hierarchy, also innate, are the *needs to know and to understand.* The need to know is the stronger of the two and must be satisfied before the need to understand appears.

Young children possess a natural curiosity about their world; they explore spontaneously and eagerly in their attempts to know and understand it. Healthy adults continue to be curious about their world. They want to analyze it and to develop a framework within which to understand it. Failure to satisfy these needs is frustrating (as is failure to satisfy any of the needs) and results in a personality which has little curiosity about things, is not involved with life, and has little zest for living. It is impossible to become self-actualizing if these needs are frustrated; if we do not know and understand the world around us, we cannot effectively interact with it to gain security, love, esteem, and fulfillment.

METAMOTIVATION: WHAT MOVES THE SELF-ACTUALIZING PERSON?

As Maslow's work with self-actualizing persons progressed, he began to suspect that these extremely healthy individuals differed both quantitatively and qualitatively from others in terms of what motivated them. This led him to propose a radical (and sometimes less than clear) theory of motivation for self-actualizing persons; he called this theory growth motivation or *metamotivation* (and it is also referred

to as Being, or B-motivation). The prefix "meta" means after or beyond, and metamotivation moves beyond the traditional idea of motivation. Paradoxically, it seems to mean a state in which motivation
plays no role at all! "The highest motive," Maslow wrote, "is to be
unmotivated and nonstriving."[4] In other words, self-actualizing
persons do not strive, they *develop*.

To understand this theory we must distinguish between the
"motivation" of self-actualizers (metamotivation) and the motivation
of others; Maslow called the latter Deficiency or D-motivation.
Deficiency motivation is motivation to make up for some deficiency in
the organism. For example, if we have gone some time without food
there is a deficit in the body. The deficit produces pain and discomfort, both physical and psychological. A tension level is induced in
the organism which it is motivated to reduce. We have a specific need
(hunger) for a specific goal object (food). Thus, this kind of motivation is designed to attain something we lack.

Apparently, although Maslow was not explicit, deficiency motivation refers not only to the physiological needs but to the needs for
safety, belonging and love, and esteem as well. These are the lower
needs and they motivate us to attain something specific which we lack.
As with the example of hunger, the needs for safety, belonging and
love, and esteem refer to specific goal objects in the environment
which will satisfy the needs and reduce the tension they generate.
Neurotics and persons of normal mental health are so motivated; they
strive for lower-need gratification.

In contrast, supremely healthy persons (self-actualizers) are
concerned with the higher needs: fulfilling their potentialities and
knowing and understanding the world around them. In this case—
metamotivation—the person is not trying to make up for deficits or
trying to reduce tension. The goal is to enrich and enlarge the
experience of living, to increase the joy and ecstasy at being alive. The
ideal is to increase tension through new, challenging, and diverse
experiences.

Since there do not seem to be specific goal objects in the environment to attain, what is the motivation of these self-actualizers? They
are not motivated in the usual sense of the term (Maslow's deficiency
motivation). Rather they are "metamotivated" to be fully human, to
be all they have the potential to be. This motivation is "character
growth, character expression, maturation, and development; in a

4. A. H. Maslow, *Motivation and Personality,* 2nd ed. (New York: Harper & Row, 1970),
    p. 135.

word self-actualization."[5] Self-actualizers are beyond striving, desiring, or wishing for something they need to correct a deficit; all their deficits have been corrected. They are no longer *becoming*, in the sense of satisfying the lower needs. Now they are in a state of *being*, of spontaneously, naturally, joyously expressing their full humanness. In that sense, then, they are unmotivated.

However, having explained all this, Maslow set forth a list of *metaneeds* which seem to constitute states of growth or being (or perhaps goals) toward which self-actualizers move. Maslow also referred to them as B-values and they are ends in themselves rather than means of achieving other ends, states of being rather than becoming or striving toward some specific goal object.

If these states exist as needs (and Maslow said they "behave like needs"[6]), failure to satisfy or achieve them would somehow be harmful, as is failure to satisfy any of the lower needs. And this is exactly what happens; frustration of the metaneeds produces *metapathology*.

The kind of illness produced by frustration of the growth needs is not experienced as explicitly as that produced by frustration of the lower needs. This does not mean that the metapathologies are not felt as keenly as ordinary illnesses, but the source or cause of the disturbance is less clear to the individual. When one of the deficit needs is frustrated (hunger or love, for example), we are directly and immediately aware of the feeling of hunger or loneliness. That is not so with frustration of the metaneeds.

We may certainly be aware that something is wrong but we do not know what it is; we do not know what we are lacking. Metapathology is a rather formless malaise; we feel alone, helpless, meaningless, depressed, and despairing, but we cannot point to something and say, "There! That person, or that object, is the cause of my feeling this way." And since we cannot point to a specific source or goal which will alleviate our distress, it becomes very difficult to deal with a metapathological state.

Perhaps this will be made clearer by presenting Maslow's metaneeds along with the specific metapathologies which result from metaneed frustration. Items in the left column of the chart on page 67 represent the states of being (B-values) of the self-actualizing person. Items in the right column represent the associated metapathologies.[7]

5. Ibid., p. 159.
6. A. H. Maslow, "Self-Actualization and Beyond," in J. F. T. Bugental, ed., *Challenges of Humanistic Psychology* (New York: McGraw-Hill, 1967), p. 281.
7. Chart adapted from A. H. Maslow, *The Farther Reaches of Human Nature* (New York: Viking, 1971), pp. 318–19.

Maslow's Metaneeds and Metapathologies

B-values	Metapathologies
Truth	Mistrust, cynicism, skepticism
Goodness	Hatred, repulsion, disgust, reliance only upon self and for self
Beauty	Vulgarity, restlessness, loss of taste, bleakness
Unity; wholeness	Disintegration
Dichotomy-transcendence	Black/white thinking, either / or thinking, simplistic view of life
Aliveness; process	Deadness, robotizing, feeling oneself to be totally determined, loss of emotion and zest in life, experiential emptiness
Uniqueness	Loss of feeling of self and individuality, feeling oneself to be interchangeable or anonymous
Perfection	Hopelessness, nothing to work for
Necessity	Chaos, unpredictability
Completion; finality	Incompleteness, hopelessness, cessation of striving and coping
Justice	Anger, cynicism, mistrust, lawlessness, total selfishness
Order	Insecurity, wariness, loss of safety and predictability, necessity for being on guard
Simplicity	Overcomplexity, confusion, bewilderment, loss of orientation
Richness, totality, comprehensiveness	Depression, uneasiness, loss of interest in the world
Effortlessness	Fatigue, strain, clumsiness, awkwardness, stiffness
Playfulness	Grimness, depression, paranoid humorlessness, loss of zest in life, cheerlessness
Self-sufficiency	Responsibility given to others
Meaningfulness	Meaninglessness, despair, senselessness of life

The metapathologies represent a diminution or thwarting of full human growth and development. Their existence prevents us from fully expressing, utilizing, and fulfilling our potential. It is important to reiterate that persons with metapathologies have satisfied the lower needs. They may love and belong, feel basically secure, and have a sense of self-esteem. The deficit needs are no longer pushing for satisfaction. Despite this, they are not healthy personalities. Healthy persons operate on a higher and a more vague or general level of motivation.

We have seen what metamotivates healthy personalities, in Maslow's view. Now let us examine specific characteristics of healthy personalities. What are self-actualizers really like?

CHARACTERISTICS OF SELF-ACTUALIZERS

We have already mentioned some general characteristics of self-actualizing persons. By definition, they have sufficiently satisfied in turn the lower needs: physiological, safety, love and belonging, and esteem. They are free of psychoses, neuroses, or other pathological disturbances. They are models of maturation and health, fulfilling themselves by using their capacities and qualities to the utmost. They know who and what they are and where they are going.

Another important general characteristic is age: self-actualizers seem to be middle-aged and older. Younger people, Maslow thought, have not developed a strong sense of identity and autonomy. They have not acquired an enduring love relationship, found a calling to devote themselves to, or developed their own values, patience, courage, and wisdom. Although young people cannot be fully actualizing, it is possible, Maslow found, for them to demonstrate "good growth toward self-actualization," healthy characteristics that seem to point the individual toward psychological maturation and health.

Although self-actualization is an instinctoid need, it is very much dependent on childhood experiences to facilitate or thwart its later development. Maslow believed that harsh domination and control of the child is harmful, as is the opposite—excessive freedom and permissiveness. The most effective child-rearing approach is "freedom within limits," a judicious mixture of control and freedom.

It is vital for later self-actualization that the child feel loved. Maslow emphasized the importance of the first two years of life; if the two-year-old has not received adequate love, security, and esteem, it will be extremely difficult for it to grow toward self-actualization.

Beyond these general points, Maslow discussed a number of specific characteristics which describe self-actualizers.

1. An Efficient Perception of Reality

Supremely healthy persons perceive objects and persons in the world around them objectively. (Maslow called this objective perception Being or B-cognition.) They do not regard the world only as they want or need it to be, but they see it as it is. As part of this objectivity in perception, Maslow found that self-actualizers are accurate judges of others, quickly able to detect fakery and dishonesty.

This accuracy extends to other aspects of life—art, music, and intellectual, political, or scientific concerns. Self-actualizers do not see such matters in terms of fashion, or the way the "best" people see them, or the way anyone else sees them. They rely solely on their own judgment and perception and this involves no biases or prejudgments.

Unhealthy personalities perceive the world in their own subjective terms, forcing it to fit the shapes of their fears, needs, and values.[8] "The neurotic is not emotionally sick," Maslow wrote, "he is cognitively *wrong!*"[9] One cannot interact and cope with the world and with other people if one has only a subjective picture of them. The more objectively we are able to reflect reality, the better is our ability to reason logically, to reach correct conclusions, and to be intellectually efficient in general.

Thus, we return to the controversy over whether psychological health is equated with subjectivity or objectivity in perception. The alternatives are extreme: if we perceive the world only in our own terms are we sick or well, neurotic or healthy? We shall meet this point again with other models of psychological health.

2. A General Acceptance of Nature, Others, and Oneself

Self-actualizing persons accept themselves, their shortcomings and their strengths, without complaint or worry. In fact, they don't think about them very much. Even these supremely healthy individuals have weaknesses and imperfections, but they do not feel shame or guilt over them. They accept their nature as it is. Maslow wrote: "One does not complain about water because it is wet, or about rocks because they are hard, or about trees because they are green."[10]

---

8. Allport (Chapter 2, pp. 6–23) and Fromm (Chapter 4, pp. 39–57) also hold this view.
9. A. H. Maslow, *Motivation and Personality*, 2nd ed. (New York: Harper & Row, 1970), p. 153.
10. Ibid., p. 156.

This is the natural order of such things, and so it is with the nature of self-actualizers.

Since they are so accepting of their natures, these healthy persons do not have to distort or falsify themselves. There is no defensiveness about them and they do not hide behind masks or social roles. They are relaxed and comfortable with themselves and this acceptance applies to all levels of existence. They accept their sensual appetites with neither shame nor apology, and they accept their levels of love and belonging, esteem, and self-worth. In general, they are equally tolerant of the shortcomings of persons they know, indeed, of the whole human species.

Maslow noted, however, that self-actualizers feel guilt, shame, worry, or regret about some aspects of their behavior, particularly discrepancies between their nature at the moment and what they could or should be. For example, they are bothered by shortcomings—in themselves or in others—that could be improved, such as laziness, thoughtlessness, jealousy, prejudice, or envy, because these weaknesses inhibit full human growth and expression.

In contrast, neurotics are crippled by shame or guilt over their weaknesses and failings, obsessed so that they divert time and energy from more constructive affairs. Even normal persons (those who are not neurotic) experience unnecessary guilt and shame about their own nature and spend too much time worrying about matters that cannot be altered.

3. Spontaneity, Simplicity, and Naturalness

In all aspects of life, self-actualizers behave in open and direct ways, devoid of pretense. They do not have to hide their emotions but can display them honestly. In simple terms, we can say that these persons behave naturally; that is, in accordance with their nature.

However, self-actualizers are also thoughtful and considerate of others. In situations where the expression of natural and honest feelings might hurt others, or where the issue is trivial, they will temporarily curb those feelings. Thus, they are not deliberately unconventional or rebellious; they take no pleasure in purposely flouting social rules and mores. And so they can play the required social games when failure to do so would hurt someone's feelings. For example, Maslow described one very healthy man who graciously accepted an honor which he privately despised. The matter wasn't important enough to make an issue of or to hurt those who sincerely felt they were rewarding and pleasing him.

However, in situations where paying obeisance to social convention interferes with what healthy persons consider to be important, they do not hesitate to defy the rules. Again, they are simply and naturally themselves, confident and secure, and unconventional without being aggressive and rebellious.

Neurotics and non-self-actualizing persons cannot function spontaneously; they must distort those aspects of themselves which cause them shame or guilt.

4. A Focus on Problems Outside Themselves

The self-actualizing persons studied by Maslow were committed to their work. Without exception they had a sense of mission which absorbed them, and to which they devoted most of their energy. So strongly did Maslow feel about this characteristic that he concluded that it is impossible to become self-actualizing without this sense of dedication.

Self-actualizing persons love their work and feel that it is naturally suited for them. Maslow described it as analogous to a perfect love affair: the work and the person seem "meant for each other . . . the person and [the] job fit together and belong together perfectly like a key and a lock."[11] Their work is something they want to do; indeed, it is something they must do, not merely a job in order to earn a living.

Through this intense dedication to their work, self-actualizers are able to achieve or fulfill the metaneeds. A writer, philosopher, or scientist may search for truth through work, an artist might search for beauty, a lawyer for justice. They do not engage in their work for money, fame, or power, but because it satisfies the metaneeds, challenges and develops their abilities, causes them to grow to the highest level of their potential, and helps define their sense of who and what they are.

As a result of this absorption in work, and of the intense satisfaction it brings, these healthy personalities work very hard, more so than those of average mental health. But of course it is not a chore to them; it is their play as well. They enjoy doing their work more than anything else, and continue doing it even if they no longer need the income it provides. Maslow noted that for these persons, ideas such as

11. A. H. Maslow, *The Farther Reaches of Human Nature* (New York: Viking, 1971), pp. 301–02.

vacation, fun, entertainment, rest, or hobby are fused into their mission, their calling, their work.

5. A Need for Privacy and Independence

Self-actualizing persons have a strong need for detachment and solitude. While they do not shrink from human contact, they do not seem to need other people. They are not dependent on others for their satisfactions and so may be aloof and reserved. Their behaviors and feelings are strongly self-centered and self-directed. This means that they have the ability to make up their own minds, reach their own decisions, and exercise their own motivation and discipline.

Neurotics, on the other hand, are usually highly emotionally dependent on others for satisfactions which they are incapable of producing for themselves. Since they do not have a strong sense of self, they lean on others for support and for ideas, values, and behaviors. They can be considered parasitic; they think and act in accordance with the fashions of others—parents, preachers, or propagandists. Their sense of self is merely a reflection of others and not a product of their own independent development.

Since self-actualizers do not depend on or cling to others and prefer privacy and solitude, they sometimes experience social difficulties. Average people may think of them as unfriendly, snobbish, perhaps even hostile. This is not the intention of healthy persons; they are not deliberately avoiding others, they simply do not have a strong need for them.

6. Autonomous Functioning

Closely related to the need for privacy and independence is the preference and ability of self-actualizers to function autonomously of the social and physical environments. Since they are no longer motivated by deficiency motives, they are not dependent on the real world for their satisfactions because satisfaction of the growth motives comes from within. Their development depends on their own potentialities and inner resources. (Love, esteem, and other lower-need satisfactions, on the other hand, depend on external sources for gratification.)

Healthy personalities are self-contained and their high degree of autonomy renders them rather impervious to crises or deprivations.

Misfortunes that might devastate less healthy persons may hardly be felt by self-actualizers; they retain a basic serenity in the midst of what less healthy persons consider catastrophes.

Less healthy persons, as noted, are highly dependent on the real world for the gratification of the deficiency motives. Anything which threatens to disrupt that dependency is frightening; without others, how could such persons function? How could they survive?

7. A Continued Freshness of Appreciation

Self-actualizers continually appreciate certain experiences, no matter how often they are repeated, with a fresh sense of pleasure, awe, and wonder. A lovely or restful view on the daily drive to work, for example, may be seen with as much pleasure after five years as it was the first day. Self-actualizers have the ability to appreciate these experiences—a sunset or a symphony, a favorite meal or their spouse's laughter—as though they were new. Some react to nature, others to children, still others to music. They do not become sated or bored by life's experiences.

As a result, they take little for granted but continue to be thankful for what they possess and can experience. Maslow noted that none of his self-actualizing subjects felt the same about going to parties or night clubs or making a lot of money. Often their joy-producing experiences were trivial, everyday activities, events less healthy persons might not even notice.

8. Mystical, or "Peak," Experiences

There are occasions when self-actualizing persons experience intense and overwhelming ecstasy, bliss, and awe akin to deep religious experiences. During these peak experiences, which Maslow found to be common among his healthy subjects, the self is transcended and the person is gripped by a feeling of power, confidence, and decisiveness, a profound sense that there is nothing he or she could not accomplish or become. In addition, the activity being engaged in is magnified to orgasmic proportions—working, enjoying music, art, or sex, or simply watching a sunset or the blossoming of a garden in spring.

Maslow pointed out that not all peak experiences are so extremely intense; there can be mild ones. These mild experiences may occur, occasionally, in all of us. The healthier individual, however, has peak experiences more often than the average person, perhaps as frequently as every day.

As Maslow continued his work on self-actualization, he came to recognize two kinds of self-actualizers: those who have many peaks of strong intensity and those who have fewer and milder peaks. Both types are supremely healthy; both are self-actualizing. But he introduced the notion of two kinds of self-actualization distinguished by the quantity and quality of the transcendent peak experiences. We might describe these types as "normal super healthy" and "super super healthy." Maslow called them "peakers" and "nonpeakers," or "transcenders" and "nontranscenders."

There are other differences between these two types of self-actualizers. Nonpeakers tend to be practical persons, effectively interacting with the real world and less with the loftier realm of B-living. They are, of course, vitally concerned with developing and using their personal capacities and potentials. They are leaders in the world for good purposes and "tend to be doers rather than meditators or contemplators, effective and pragmatic rather than aesthetic, reality-testing and cognitive rather than emotional and experiencing."[12] Maslow cited Eleanor Roosevelt as an example of this kind of psychological health, and possibly presidents Truman and Eisenhower.

Peakers live more in the B-realm, are more clearly metamotivated, and have peak experiences which provide illuminating insights about themselves and their world. They tend to be more mystical, poetic, and religious, are more responsive to beauty, and are more likely to be innovators and discoverers. Less practical than nonpeakers, peakers have transcended to a greater degree everyday concerns and may seem to others as almost saintly. Maslow noted that Aldous Huxley, Albert Schweitzer, and Albert Einstein were examples of this higher level of psychological health.

However, Maslow was quite insistent that peakers are not all mystics, artists, or scientists. He found peakers among business executives, educators, and politicians, although he noted that many people find this hard to believe.

9. Social Interest

Self-actualizers possess strong and deep feelings of empathy and affection for all human beings, as well as a desire to help humanity.

12. Ibid., p. 281.

They are members of a single family—the human race—and have a feeling of brotherhood with every other member of the family. This is a special kind of brotherhood, like the attitude of an older brother or sister toward younger siblings.

It cannot be said that self-actualizers feel a kinship with all persons. Indeed, because they differ in significant ways from average persons they realize that they function on a higher level. As with older brothers and sisters, these supremely healthy persons know they can achieve things better than others and that they see and understand things more clearly. Thus, just as one can love and identify with younger brothers and sisters, so self-actualizers love humankind. They may often be depressed or angered by the foolish, weak, or cruel behavior of others, but they are quick to understand and to forgive.

10. Interpersonal Relations

Self-actualizers are capable of stronger relationships with others than are persons of average mental health. They are capable of greater love, deeper friendship, and more complete identification with other individuals. However, their interpersonal relationships, while more intense, are fewer in number than those of non-self-actualizers. After all, there are so few supremely healthy persons from whom to pick friends, colleagues, and spouses, and self-actualizers, like most persons, prefer to be with those who share their values and characteristics.

While the circle of persons they are close to is thus small, self-actualizers are nonetheless kind and patient toward others, particularly children. However, while they have compassion and love for humanity in general, they can be harsh and, infrequently, cruel to those who are hypercritical, pretentious, or pompous. This occasional hostility toward some individuals does not lessen their general compassion for the human race.

The love self-actualizers feel toward another person is of a special kind: Being love (B-love), as opposed to Deficiency love (D-love). Deficiency love is motivated by deficiency needs, specifically by the lack of satisfaction of the belonging and love needs. There is strong dependence on the loved one and fear of losing the love that is needed so desperately. Persons of average mental health, when deprived of love, crave it as a hungry person craves, begs, and needs food.

In B-love, the healthy person, not suffering a deficiency, does not crave love and may do without it for periods of time. Since healthy persons do not have a high degree of dependence on the loved one, they experience no fear or jealousy. Theirs is an unselfish love in which giving love is at least as important as receiving it, and in which one cares for the growth and development of the other person as much as for one's own growth. There is much fun, joy, laughter, and happiness in B-love, qualities lacking in deficiency-motivated love.

11.   A Democratic Character Structure

Supremely healthy persons tolerate and accept all people regardless of social class, level of education, political or religious affiliation, race, or color. Such differences do not matter to self-actualizers. Indeed, Maslow suspected that they are seldom aware of these differences.

But their behavior goes deeper than tolerance. In their relations with others—for example, with those of less education or intelligence—they do not maintain a posture of superiority. They are quite ready to listen to and learn from anyone who can teach them something. The self-actualizing intellectual, for example, is genuinely respectful toward the skilled carpenter because the carpenter displays skills and knowledge that the intellectual does not possess.

12.   Discrimination Between Means and Ends, Between Good and Evil

Self-actualizers clearly distinguish between means and ends. For them, the ends or goals are much more important than the means of reaching them. However, this is more complicated because self-actualizers often consider as ends in themselves certain activities and experiences that are means for less healthy persons. What Maslow seems to be pointing out is that fully healthy persons enjoy "doing" or "getting there" as much as or more than achieving the goal or arriving. The means become ends because of the enjoyment and satisfaction they bring.

Self-actualizers are also able to distinguish between good and evil, right and wrong. Less healthy persons are often confused or inconsistent in ethical dealings, vacillating or alternating between right and wrong in terms of expedience. In contrast, self-actualizers have well-defined ethical and moral standards to which they adhere in all situations.

13. An Unhostile Sense of Humor

Fully healthy persons differ from average individuals in what they find humorous, in what makes them laugh. Less healthy persons laugh at three kinds of humor: hostile humor which involves someone being hurt, superiority humor which takes advantage of the inferiority of another person or group, and authority-rebellion humor relating to an Oedipal situation or to smut.

The humor of self-actualizers is philosophical; it involves making fun of humanity in general but never of a specific individual. It is often instructive, designed to make a point as well as produce a laugh. It is a thoughtful kind of humor which results in a smile and a nod of understanding rather than in loud laughter. This kind of humor is appreciated only by other equally healthy persons. Average individuals do not, as a rule, find self-actualizers very funny and are apt to walk away from them wondering why they are so somber and serious.

14. Creativeness

Creativeness is a characteristic one would expect of self-actualizing persons. They are original, inventive, and innovative, although not always in terms of producing an artistic creation; they are not all writers, artists, or composers. Maslow compared this creativeness to the naive inventiveness and imagination children possess, an unbiased and direct way of looking at things. Most of us lose this childhood creativeness under the pressure of school and other social forces, but self-actualizers retain it or regain it later in life.

Creativeness, then, is more of an attitude, an expression of psychological health, and is concerned more with the way we perceive and react to the world than with finished products of an artistic nature. Thus, persons in any occupation can display creativeness.

15. Resistance to Enculturation

Self-actualizers are self-sufficient and autonomous, well able to resist social pressures to think or act in certain ways. They maintain an inner detachment, an aloofness from their culture, guided by themselves rather than by others.

However, they are not openly rebellious against the culture. They do not deliberately violate social rules to demonstrate independence. Indeed, they can be quite conventional with regard to dress, decorum, or any other matter they consider trivial. Only when an issue arises of great personal importance (usually a moral or ethical matter) will they openly challenge the rules and norms of society.

This formidable list of personal qualities may seem like an exaggeration or caricature of even the healthiest personality; surely no one could be that saintly, at least not for long periods of time. Rest easy—Maslow's portrait of the healthy personality is more realistic than that. Self-actualizers are, after all, human beings. They are not perfect, just closer to perfection than most others.

Maslow found that self-actualizers can at times be silly, thoughtless, stubborn, irritating, vain, ruthless, and temperamental, characteristics shared with less healthy individuals. Also, they are not totally free of guilt, anxiety, shame, worry, or conflict. However, these imperfections are experienced much less frequently by healthy persons than by less healthy ones.

A PERSONAL COMMENT

It is easy to see why Maslow's work made him such a recognized and respected leader in the human potential movement. His appealing personal characteristics come through so clearly on the pages of his books; here was a man who deeply cared for the human race and who saw in it the best rather than the worst. But there is more to his acceptance than his personal qualities. Maslow offered an optimistic theory of human nature, pointing out what all of us are capable of becoming. His self-actualizing person is a flattering portrait of the best of humanity.

I find myself very much wanting to believe this theory. Who wouldn't want to believe that we are capable of so much more than the violence and injustice we read in our daily newspapers and watch on our television screens? Maslow himself undertook his work in the belief that there are such noble capabilities in all of us. "I wanted to prove that human beings are capable of something grander than war and prejudice and hatred."[13]

However, in spite of wanting to embrace Maslow's theory in all its details and ramifications, I find myself questioning certain aspects. Does every human being truly have the potential to be an Olympic Gold Medal winner, to use Maslow's analogy? Do we all possess the possibility of approaching that level of performance?

13. M. H. Hall, "Conversation with Abraham H. Maslow," *Psychology Today*, 1968, 2, p. 55.

Obviously, some people do; gold medals are awarded. And Maslow did find persons whom he thought to be supremely healthy. But he found so few of them that I consider this a point of concern (and disappointment)—that a need alleged to be universal is so seldom satisfied or achieved. Maslow did offer some explanation as to why the state of self-actualization is so seldom reached. It could be that most of us have unfortunate childhood experiences which, he said, can inhibit self-actualization. Also, becoming self-actualizing involves a lot of hard work, courage, and persistence; he thought this could account for its infrequency. And of course, as the highest need, self-actualization is also the weakest.

Another question I have involves Maslow's criteria for selecting the self-actualizing persons he studied. He did not note explicitly what those criteria were. The persons seemed to be ones he admired greatly. Did he choose them, or was he biased in his selection, by what these admirable men and women had achieved and contributed to society? This is a question that cannot be answered.

These points, although troubling to me, do not negate Maslow's basic thesis that some persons (however few) are exemplary models of psychological health. Surely such persons exist. Further, the point that we can learn what constitutes psychological health only by studying the best representatives of the species (what Maslow called the "growing tip" of humanity) should serve as the foundation for future research on the healthy personality.

Maslow's hierarchy of needs is appealing to me, particularly his insistence that the physiological and safety needs be satisfied before other needs can appear. With regard to the love and esteem needs, their order might be reversed for those who value esteem more than love, a possibility which Maslow admitted. Every theory which posits universals of behavior or motivation seems to have exceptions, and Maslow's theory is no exception to this rule. Indeed, there are persons who behave in ways quite opposite to his hierarchy; a person who fasts to death for a cause in which he or she believes is denying physiological and safety needs in favor of some higher need. Despite these few exceptions, however, I think the hierarchy concept is a reasonable one.

A question has been raised as to whether self-actualization is elitist, reserved for the more intelligent, better educated, and more affluent members of society. How might a person with little education, marginally employed in a series of dead-end jobs, with no prospects for a better future, aspire to the fortunate state of self-actualization? It seems to me that such a person might never be able to rise above the physiological and safety needs. Are we more likely to find self-actualizing in the executive suite or the suburbs than in the factory or the ghetto?

Since it is impossible to become self-actualizing without a commitment to work, one's job or career can inhibit or support the attempt at self-actualization. The kind of work which would seem to foster self-actualization is that which persons are free to perform in their own way, unlike an assembly line where workers have little say in what they do, how they do it, or the speed at which they must work.

I feel that few jobs in Western technological societies today offer opportunity for creative expression, autonomy, and the fulfillment of the higher needs. Is this another reason why there are so few self-actualizing persons? Too many of us work in assembly-line fashion, processing fenders, memoranda, students, or patients, and our jobs quickly become routine, devoid of challenge or the chance to develop and fulfill our potentials.

Opportunities for self-actualization could also be limited by economic conditions. Certainly in a severe economic depression (such as the 1930s) it is enough of a problem for many people to survive physically from day to day. In times of affluence, however, such as the late 1960s and early 1970s, satisfying physiological and safety needs is relatively easy. It is significant that the human potential movement blossomed during that time of affluence, particularly among middle-class young people. Unconcerned with money or safety, they were free to give thought to enriching and enlarging their lives.

However, the notion that self-actualization might be curtailed by economic conditions or by one's level of opportunity does not detract from Maslow's thesis. If anything, these points support the notion of a hierarchy of needs and the necessity of satisfying lower needs before higher needs become apparent.

Maslow's distinction between deficiency and growth motivation is intuitively and rationally appealing, as is the notion that persons, once self-actualizing, operate on a higher level of motivation. Self-actualizers do seem to be beyond striving or desiring something specific, instead developing and becoming in a natural, almost inevitable, unfolding of their potential.

Maslow's concept of metapathology seems to offer a reasonable explanation of why those persons who appear to have everything (security, love, esteem, success) are miserable. It is because they cannot point to a lack of something specific in their lives. In my work with successful, middle-class, middle-aged individuals I see evidence of this general malaise. These persons have not yet taken that extra step toward satisfaction of the metaneeds. They haven't yet expressed their full development and have potentials which are not in use. Having satisfied lower needs, they feel the need for self-actualization exerting its pull.

Maslow's characteristics of self-actualizers are those one would hope and expect a healthy person to possess. Certainly we might wish to possess them ourselves. The ideals seem worth developing. Self-actualizers are kind, decent, honest, caring persons and society might well be a more fit place in which to live if more of us displayed these characteristics. And we might as individuals be happier if we were around more self-actualizing persons (and followed their example).

These supremely healthy persons seem perfect in many ways: in their understanding and accepting of themselves and others, in their naturalness and spontaneity, in their concern and compassion for humanity, in their tolerance of others, and in their ability to resist social pressures.

Yet they have distinctly human (less than perfect) characteristics as well. They are bothered by their imperfections and by those of others. They want everyone to be fully human, actualizing, and fulfilling, and are disturbed when others are not. They can be vain, petty, and thoughtless, just like less healthy persons.

Perhaps most of us feel that there should be more to life, that we are not functioning on as high a level as we are capable, that we are not fully in use. Most of us probably experience vague feelings of discontent because we believe we could be better than we are. Maslow's hierarchy of needs offers the challenge of climbing to a higher rung on the ladder of human growth, and it holds out the tantalizing hope that, if we are fortunate in our circumstances, we might have a chance of reaching self-actualization, or at least of getting close.

BIBLIOGRAPHY

Hall, M. H. A conversation with Abraham H. Maslow. *Psychology Today,* 1968, 2, 34–37, 54–57.

Maddi, S. R., and Costa, P. T. *Humanism in Personology: Allport, Maslow, and Murray.* Chicago: Aldine-Atherton, 1972.

Maslow, A. H. Self-Actualization and Beyond. In J. F. T. Bugental, ed., *Challenges of Humanistic Psychology.* New York: McGraw-Hill, 1967, pp. 279–86.

——. *Toward a Psychology of Being,* 2nd ed. New York: D. Van Nostrand, 1968.

——. *Motivation and Personality,* 2nd ed. New York: Harper & Row, 1970.

——. *The Farther Reaches of Human Nature.* New York: Viking, 1971.

6

The individuated person
Jung's model

In 1913, when Carl Jung (1875–1961) was thirty-eight years old, he thought he was going insane. For the next three years he felt disoriented, "totally suspended in midair," under a constant state of inner pressure, lonely, and burdened by torments he could mention to no one, for fear he would be misunderstood.

At this time in his life Jung was an established and respected psychiatrist with a large private practice, a wife and family, and a lectureship at the University of Zurich in Switzerland. On the surface he had a richly rewarding personal and professional life. Just a few months earlier he had broken a close emotional and professional tie with Sigmund Freud (a difficult event for both men); however, that rupture did not seem to be the sole cause of Jung's problems. For some reason, he felt his life lacked meaning or zest. His intellectual activities came to a halt; he wrote very little and was unable to read scientific books. He gave up his university career, resigning his lectureship because he felt he could not teach when his own intellectual and emotional situation was so confused and worrisome.

Jung felt in danger of losing contact with the real world but, fortunately, the needs of his patients and family provided enough exposure to his normal life that he was able to continue. It was very difficult. He had to keep reminding himself who and what he was. "I have a medical diploma from a Swiss university, I must help my patients, I have a wife and five children, I live at 228 Seestrasse in Kusnacht—these were actualities that made demands upon me and proved to me again and again that I really existed, that I was not a blank page whirling about in the winds of the spirit."[1]

In this turmoil, Jung began to examine his life, particularly his

1. C. G. Jung, *Memories, Dreams, Reflections* (New York: Vintage Books, 1961), p. 189.

childhood, in the hope of recognizing some incident which might have caused his disturbance. He reviewed his life twice and found nothing. Finally, he gave up trying to understand his problem on an intellectual level and resolved to do whatever occurred to him, no matter how nonsensical it might be. He surrendered himself to the impulses of his unconscious, a process he later formalized as the *confrontation with the unconscious.*

The first thing his unconscious led him to do was build a model village out of small stones, a re-creation of a period in his childhood when he had played passionately with building blocks. "There is still life in these things," he thought as he searched for stones. "The small boy is still around."[2] He was obsessed with his new activity, spending as much time at it as he possibly could. At first he resisted because it seemed so humiliating. Was there nothing for him to do but play the games of his childhood? But he later realized that "this moment was a turning point in my fate."[3]

The building of toy villages out of stones was only the beginning of Jung's confrontation with his unconscious. Fantasies and dreams were released by this activity and Jung followed them actively and eagerly during the next years.

The confrontation worked. Out of this prolonged journey into the unconscious, Jung fashioned a new meaning and center for his own life and a new understanding of the human personality. His writings leave no doubt of the importance of this experience. His unfolding unconscious was like a "stream of lava, and the heat of its fires reshaped my life. . . . The years when I was pursuing my inner images were the most important of my life—in them everything essential was decided."[4] Not surprisingly, Jung's conception of psychological health emerged from this intensely personal experience.[5]

Jung had long been aware of the importance of the inner world of dreams and fantasies, and as an old man he could describe dreams, with sparkling clarity and detail, that he had experienced as early as

2. Ibid., p. 174.
3. Ibid., p. 174.
4. Ibid., p. 199.
5. Evidence suggests that Freud also underwent a profound emotional crisis in his early forties (two decades before his rupture with Jung). During Freud's midlife crisis he was "probably more troubled than in any other decade of his life" and suffered from urinary irritability, anxiety, migraine headaches, and the cessation of his sex life which occurred at the age of forty-one [P. Roazen, *Freud and His Followers*, New York: Knopf, 1975, pp. 82–83, 51–52]. Freud apparently resolved his crisis in the same way that Jung did, by confronting his unconscious. Freud analyzed his own dreams, a process he described in *The Interpretation of Dreams*, published in 1900.

age three. He had been a lonely, isolated child of neurotic parents and for years his sole companion was a wooden figure he had carved himself. To escape his parents and their marital problems, he spent hours in the attic of his childhood home playing with and confiding in the wooden figure. Cut off as he was from the external world, he focused on his own world of myths, dreams, visions, and fantasies.

Jung felt that at crucial times in his youth the solutions to problems or the proper choice among alternatives were determined for him by manifestations of his unconscious in dreams or visions. For example, when it was time to begin his university studies he was racked with indecision about a specialty. Then, in a dream, he saw himself unearthing bones of prehistoric animals in an ancient burial mound. This settled the matter; he would study nature and science in accordance with his interpretation of the dream.

That dream, in which Jung was digging beneath the surface, plus a dream he had had at three years of age in which he was in a huge underground cavern, may have presaged the direction of his study of the human personality—underground, beneath the surface. And what is beneath the surface of the personality? The unconscious.

We have noted with other theorists how personal experiences may have shaped their understanding of personality. This relationship between personal experience and professional approach may be even stronger with Jung. His definition of and prescription for psychological health is a mirror image of his own emotional crisis and the way in which he resolved it. He fashioned an elaborate theory of personality, totally unlike any other, focusing on the necessity of each individual confronting and heeding unconscious experiences.

Jung's intriguing blend of psychology, mysticism, and the occult has found a large and enthusiastic audience, particularly among young people. This audience continues to grow as more people become interested in Eastern religions, existentialism, and the supernatural—points of view congenial with Jung's work. Despite the fact that his books are difficult to read, Jung's work seems more popular today than at the time of his death in 1961.

The form and focus of Jung's view of the healthy personality have little in common with other theorists. His work stands apart, solitary, as Jung himself remained all his life.

JUNG'S APPROACH TO PERSONALITY

More than any other theorist, Jung placed a strong emphasis on the unconscious. Sigmund Freud first awakened us to the importance of unconscious forces in shaping personality, but Jung gave a deeper dimension to that hidden, inner life we all possess. Jung included as part of the unconscious not only the experiences that each of us accumulates in life, but also the experiences that all members of the human species and their animal ancestors have accumulated. In a very real sense, we each possess a built-in heritage composed of all the experiences of all human beings for all time.

Through observations of his patients, voracious reading of myths and legends of ancient civilizations (their symbols, rituals, and religions), and explorations into such diverse topics as alchemy, astrology, and clairvoyance, Jung charted the nature of the all-powerful, far-ranging unconscious. His own experience during his midlife crisis (and the experiences of many of his patients) also persuaded him of the necessity of regaining contact with the symbols, rituals, and myths of human history as contained in the unconscious.

Much human misery and despair, and feelings of senselessness, aimlessness, and meaninglessness result, Jung argued, from loss of contact with the unconscious foundations of the personality. He believed that much of that lost contact is due to our increasing belief in science and reason as guides to living. We have become too one-sided, he said, stressing the conscious, rational being at the expense of the unconscious.[6]

We have freed ourselves from superstitious beliefs (or so we try to persuade ourselves) but, in the process, we have lost our spiritual values and our identity with nature; in other words, we have become dehumanized. And so we feel ourselves to be without meaning or connection, overcome by futility and emptiness. This "general neurosis of our time" is a direct result of the loss of our spiritual connection with our past. It is a sickness of dissociation and disorganization and there is only one cure: a renewal of contact with the unconscious forces of our personalities. Thus, Jung's prescription for humanity is precisely what it was for himself—a confrontation with the unconscious.

Jung was not arguing for the domination or control of the personality by the unconscious. Quite the opposite; his ideal of psychological health was conscious direction and guidance of the unconscious forces. The worlds of the conscious and unconscious must be integrated; both sides must be allowed to develop freely.

6. There is a striking parallel between this view of Jung's and a comment by Carl Rogers decades later: "The tragic condition of man is that he has lost confidence in his own nonconscious inner directions." [C. R. Rogers, "Actualizing tendency in relation to motives and to consciousness," in M. R. Jones, ed., *Nebraska Symposium on Motivation, 1963* (Lincoln: University of Nebraska Press, 1963), p. 21.]

The process by which this integration of the personality takes place is *individuation,* or self-realization. This process of "coming to selfhood" is a natural one. Indeed, it is so strong a tendency that Jung considered it to be an instinct. Yet, there are many obstacles to attaining individuation and Jung was not optimistic that everyone was capable of doing so. Those who do can achieve the ultimate in selfhood, understanding, psychological maturity and health, wholeness, and full humanness. This goal of human existence must be striven for but it is rarely reached until middle age, the time when Jung underwent his own personal crisis and resolution.

In order to understand what Jung meant by individuation, we have to examine his views on the structure of the personality and how it changes over time.

THE STRUCTURE OF THE PERSONALITY

In Jung's view, the personality is composed of three separate but interacting systems: the ego, the personal unconscious, and the collective unconscious. Although these systems differ, they are nonetheless capable of influencing one another.

The collective unconscious is the most important part of the personality and it is also the most controversial aspect of Jung's entire theory. We will discuss the two lesser systems first.

The *ego* is the conscious mind and it includes all the perceptions, memories, thoughts, and feelings which are in our awareness at any moment. We are, throughout life, continually bombarded by a wide range of stimuli, too many for us to effectively attend to. Therefore, we must be selective in our perception of what goes on around us. We must filter out stimuli which are meaningless, irrelevant, and trivial, as well as those which are harmful or threatening. The ego performs this vital function. Unless a sensation, idea, or memory is recognized and admitted to consciousness by the ego, it will not be seen or heard or thought.

Much of our consciousness (how we perceive and react to the world) is determined by the *attitudes* of *extraversion* and *introversion*. These represent opposing ways of looking at the world and they are the most well-known part of Jung's theory. In general, they have been well accepted by psychology as a whole. They represent two different orientations of consciousness, two personality types with which we are all familiar.

A person whose attitude is extraversion is oriented toward the

external world of objective reality. Such a person is open and sociable with others and seems genuinely to enjoy the company of other persons. The introvert, on the other hand, is oriented toward an inner, subjective life and is likely to be introspective, withdrawn, and shy. These two attitudes represent opposing directions—external versus internal—and Jung felt that all human beings could be placed in one or the other category.

Normally in a person's life one of these attitudes assumes dominance and comes to rule behavior and consciousness. This does not mean that the other attitude is completely negated. It still exists but not as part of consciousness. It becomes part of the personal unconscious, where it is still capable of influencing behavior.

Thus, while a person may be basically extraverted or introverted, he or she is not completely so. The nondominant attitude is present although its influence is weaker. We shall discuss later the implications of this attitude dominance for psychological health and how it may change with age.

There is more to consciousness than extraversion or introversion. Jung also introduced the *psychological functions*. These too are ways of perceiving and reacting to the world around us and within us; that is, our external and internal worlds.

Jung discovered that not all introverts or extraverts are alike; they differ in that their attitude toward the world may be in rational or nonrational terms. Rational functions are *thinking* and *feeling*. These are actually opposing functions, but both involve making judgments and evaluations about experiences and organizing and categorizing them. Nonrational functions are *sensing* and *intuiting* and they do not involve the use of reason. These are also opposing functions in that sensing involves experiencing reality through the senses while intuiting is based on hunches or some kind of nonsensory experience.

In terms of our basic orientation to the world, only one function is dominant in consciousness and the other three become part of the personal unconscious, just as only one attitude is dominant. It is obvious that only a rational or a nonrational function can be dominant in a person because of their incompatibility. A person could not react consistently to the world using both types of function at the same time. Also, only one of each pair of functions can be dominant at any time. A person cannot operate in both the thinking and feeling modes or both the sensing and intuiting modes at the same time.

Finally, in this rather complex classification of personalities, the two attitudes and four functions interact to form eight *psychological types*. Introverted or extraverted persons can be governed by one of

four functions. For example, an introvert can function in the thinking mode or an extravert in the sensing mode.

Consciousness, while important, was considered by Jung to be of far less significance in the personality than the unconscious. There are two levels to the unconscious: the personal unconscious and the collective unconscious. The higher and more superficial level is the *personal unconscious*, essentially a storehouse or reservoir of material which is no longer conscious but which can easily rise to the conscious. This material consists of memories and thoughts which have been pushed out of conscious awareness because they are unimportant or threatening.

There is a limit to how many experiences we can be conscious of at any given time. We can only attend to or think of one or a few ideas and experiences at any moment. Other memories and thoughts have to be pushed aside to make room for the material which is currently in focus. For example, we all carry around a great deal of information—telephone numbers, addresses, names, images, and memories of events in our past. We know our telephone number but we don't think about it all the time. When we need it, however, we can recall it to conscious awareness instantly.

Thus, there is considerable traffic back and forth between the conscious and the personal unconscious. Your attention may shift from the contents of this chapter to the memory of what you did last night or the plans for what you will do tomorrow. We can compare the personal unconscious to a filing cabinet which contains all of our feelings, thoughts, and memories. It takes little effort to extract a particular memory, examine it for a while, and then put it back and forget it until the next time we are reminded of it.

An important aspect of the personal unconscious is what Jung called *complexes*, clusters of emotions, memories, and thoughts around a common theme. In a sense, complexes are smaller personalities within the total personality and are characterized by a strong preoccupation with something. For example, if we say a person has an inferiority complex or a power complex we mean that he or she is preoccupied with inferiority or power and this focus strongly influences his or her behavior.

The person with a complex, however, is not aware of how much he or she is controlled by it because it is not part of conscious awareness; the complex is in the personal unconscious. Complexes determine virtually everything about us—how we perceive the world and what values, interests, and motivations we hold.

Jung initially believed that complexes originate in traumatic childhood events, but he later came to realize that they derive from

much deeper experiences. He felt that complexes are influenced by certain experiences in the evolutionary history of the species, experiences that are transmitted from one generation to the next through hereditary mechanisms. Just as each of us has accumulated and filed all of our past experiences, so has the human species. The storehouse of these universal evolutionary experiences is the deepest and most inaccessible level of the personality, the *collective unconscious*, and it becomes the basis of an individual's personality. The collective unconscious directs all present behavior and is thus the most powerful force in the personality.

We must remember, however, that these early human experiences are unconscious; we are not aware of them. We do not consciously remember them or image them (as we can the contents of the personal unconscious which were once conscious). Instead, these early experiences exist in each of us as predispositions or tendencies to perceive, think, and feel in the same ways as did our ancestors.

Whether these tendencies are actualized or realized in our behavior depends on specific experiences we might have. For example, our primitive ancestors feared the darkness and so we inherit a predisposition to behave in the same way. This does not mean that each of us automatically grows up fearing the darkness. It means that it is easier for us to learn to fear darkness than to fear daylight. The tendency exists and needs only the right experience (say, waking from a nightmare in the dark) to make the predisposition a reality. Jung wrote: "The form of the world into which he is born is already inborn in him as a virtual image."[7] Therefore, we are predisposed to react to the world in the ways our ancestors reacted to the world.

As another example, according to Jung's theory, we are born with a predisposition to perceive our mother in a certain way. Assuming that she behaves generally as mothers behaved in past generations, our predisposition will correspond with the reality we experience. The nature of our world as inborn in us predisposes the way we perceive and react to our experiences.

Jung found these shared experiences and similar themes and symbols in his exploration of diverse cultures from all parts of the world and in all time periods. He also found these themes repeated in the fantasies and dreams of his patients. This correspondence between ancient and present is what led him to believe that certain experiences have been imprinted in the psyche because they have been repeated over so many generations.

7. C. G. Jung, *Two Essays on Analytical Psychology* (New York: Pantheon, 1953), p. 188. (Bollingen Series xx, Collected Works of C. G. Jung, Vol. 7.)

These universal experiences are manifested or expressed in us as images, which Jung called *archetypes*. By definition, an archetype is the original pattern after which a thing is made. It is a model or prototype for the fashioning of later images. Jung identified and discussed many archetypes in the course of his work; for example, birth, death, power, god, the demon, and the earth mother. There are as many archetypes as there are typical, repetitive experiences in human history.

There is one point to reiterate about archetypes: they are not fully developed memories or pictures in our minds which we can "see" clearly. We are not conscious of them. They influence us as tendencies, predispositions existing at an unconscious level.

Of all the possible archetypes, Jung believed that a few were of particular significance in our lives. They are the more fully developed and potent. These include the persona, the anima and animus, the shadow, and the self.

The word *persona* was used originally to refer to a mask worn by an actor to portray a different face or role to an audience. Jung used the word with the same meaning; the persona is a mask we wear (or hide behind) to present ourselves as something other than we are. It is the same as playing a role, adopting certain behaviors and attitudes to fit the requirements of different situations or different people.

We play many roles in life; we wear many masks. A judge presiding over the court wears one mask, but at lunch with his mistress he wears a different one. He changes again at a convention or at home with his family, adapting to what he considers appropriate in each situation, behaving how he thinks other persons expect him to behave.

Since we all play such games, the wearing of different masks seems not too harmful. Indeed, Jung believed that the persona can be useful, even necessary, to help us cope with the various events of modern life.

However, the persona can be very harmful. If a person comes to believe that the persona truly reflects his or her own nature, he or she is no longer merely playing a role but has come to be that role. As a result, the person's ego identifies solely with the persona and other facets of the personality are not allowed to fully develop. The person is alienated from his or her true self and tension develops between the inflated persona and the other deflated aspects of the personality. This is not a condition conducive to psychological health. Jung found that such persons often realize (usually around middle age) that they have been living a lie all their lives, deceiving themselves by not allowing expression of their true selves.

The goal of a healthy personality is to deflate the persona and let the rest of the personality develop. Of course, all role playing is deceit. The difference between healthy and unhealthy persons is that the latter deceive themselves as well as others. Healthy persons know when they are playing roles and, at the same time, they know their own true inner nature.

A pair of related archetypes is the *anima* and *animus*. Each of us possesses biological and psychological qualities and characteristics of the other sex. On the biological level, each sex secretes hormones of the other sex; on the psychological level, each person may behave in masculine or feminine ways. In other words, the personality of a woman contains masculine components (the archetype animus) and the personality of a man contains feminine components (the archetype anima).

These archetypes developed from the experiences of countless generations of men and women living together, in the process of which each sex acquired some of the characteristics of the other. Through these archetypes we are able to understand, to some degree, persons of the other sex. We are predisposed to like certain of their attributes and this helps us in living with and adjusting to the members of the other sex.

The importance of these archetypes for psychological health is that both must be expressed in each of us. That is, a man must express his feminine characteristics (such as tenderness) and a woman must express her masculine characteristics (such as aggressiveness), while at the same time expressing the characteristics of his or her own sex. A healthy personality cannot be achieved unless a person can express both sides of his or her nature. If such expression is not achieved, the vital other-sex characteristics will lie dormant and undeveloped, and thus a portion of the personality remains inhibited and one-sided. And the single quality which can undermine psychological health, in Jung's view, is the thwarting of full development and expression of all facets of personality. All aspects must develop harmoniously; none must grow at the expense of the others.

The *shadow* is the most powerful and potentially harmful archetype. It has the deepest roots because it contains the primitive animal instincts from our prehuman ancestry. It is a particularly troublesome archetype because it encompasses the best as well as the worst aspects of human nature, both of which must be expressed.

On the negative side, the shadow contains all the impulses that society considers evil, sinful, and immoral. As such, the shadow is our dark side and it must be tamed if we are to get along harmoniously with others. If we don't suppress these animalistic, primitive impulses, we are likely to run afoul of the mores and laws of our society. Therefore, in order to become civilized human beings we must tame these forces in the shadow, but if we totally suppress them we may reduce or destroy the desirable qualities it possesses. The shadow is not only the source of animal instincts, it is also the wellspring of spontaneity, creativity, insight, and deep emotion, all characteristics necessary for full humanness. When the shadow is fully suppressed, the personality becomes dull and lifeless, cut off from the instinctual wisdom of the past, a source of experience that Jung considered extremely valuable.

It is not desirable, then, to suppress the shadow totally, only enough to civilize a person's behavior and allow for the expression of the shadow's positive side. Again we see that one side or aspect of the personality cannot be overly repressed or developed to the exclusion of the other. There must be a harmonious blend or balance between opposites, and this feature, as we have seen, forms the basis of Jung's view of the healthy personality.

When the ego is able to regulate the forces of the shadow, allowing equal expression of both aspects, the person is lively, vigorous, and zestful. Emotions and consciousness are intensified and the person is alert and responsive in both mental and physical spheres. Jung believed that the expression of some animal instincts in a balanced shadow explains why highly creative people seem so fully alive, bursting with animal vitality.

When the shadow is totally suppressed, not only is the personality flat and dull but the person also faces the possibility of a revolt from the dark side of his or her nature. The evil, animal instincts do not disappear when they are suppressed; they lie dormant, awaiting a crisis or weakness in the ego so that they can regain control. When that happens, the individual is dominated by the unconscious, clearly not the healthiest condition.

The most important archetype is the *self*. Jung considered it to be the ultimate goal of life. The self represents striving toward unity, integration, and wholeness of all facets of the personality. When the self is developed, a person feels in harmony with his or her self and the world. An undeveloped or poorly developed self leaves the personality disjointed and precludes the attainment of full psychological health.

The archetype of self seems to represent a bringing together and balancing of all parts of the personality, an assimilation of conscious and unconscious processes such that the center of the personality shifts from the ego to a point midway between the conscious and the unconscious. Thus, material from the unconscious becomes a more active part of the personality.

The full realization or actualization of the self is a difficult, arduous, and lengthy task and is rarely achieved completely. It remains for most of us a goal to be constantly striven for but seldom reached. Thus, the self serves as a motivating force; since it always lies in the future, it pulls the person ahead.

One requirement for self-realization is to obtain objective knowledge about one's self. It is not possible, Jung wrote, to fulfill oneself without first knowing the full nature of the self. This is one reason why self-realization takes so long to approach; knowledge of one's self requires discipline, patience, persistence, and many years of hard work.

Another requisite for self-realization is the full emergence and development of all other systems of the personality, and this does not take place until middle age. Thus we see that middle age is the crucial stage of human growth for achieving psychological health, as it was in Jung's own life.

THE DEVELOPMENT OF PERSONALITY

Many psychological theorists, perhaps taking their cue from Freud, believed that the development of the human personality ceases by the age of five or so. In this view, the form and nature of personality is determined by what a person experienced in infancy and early childhood, and there is little possiblity of changing the personality after that time. A few theorists agreed that the personality might continue to develop as late as adolescence, but whether the personality is formed and crystallized by age five or fifteen, how we are formed in our early years shapes our nature for the rest of our lives. Young adulthood, middle age, or old age were seen as little more than times of elaboration or further solidification of the personality already formed.

Jung was the first theorist to take issue with this approach and to suggest that personality continues to develop throughout a person's life, and that it undergoes a crucial transformation between the ages of thirty-five and fifty.[8] This view should give hope to those yet to face this time of transition as well as to those currently in the throes of the middle-age crisis. At least we are not condemned to be prisoners of early childhood experiences.

8. Maslow also recognized the importance of middle age, but Jung's work was proposed considerably before Maslow's.

Jung described personality development over four stages: childhood, youth and young adulthood, middle age, and old age. He did not believe that the *childhood* stage of development was especially significant in the formation of personality. The infant's behavior is dominated by instincts and there are no psychological problems during this early period because problems require the existence of a conscious ego which, at that time, has not yet been formed. The infant is concerned with little more than filling the stomach, emptying bowels and bladder, and sleeping.

The ego begins to develop during childhood, initially in a rudimentary way, but the child has no unique self or identity. The child's "personality" is no more than a reflection of the personality of its parents. Thus, parents play a role in personality formation and can, through their behavior toward the child, impede the full development of the personality. The parents may, for example, try to force their own personality on the child, wanting it to be an extension of themselves. Or they may expect the child to be totally different, hoping to find a vicarious compensation for their own deficiencies.

The second stage in personality development, *youth and young adulthood,* begins at puberty when the personality begins to develop a definite form and content. Jung referred to puberty as the "psychic birth" of the individual and it is a time of many problems, conflicts, and adaptations. The real world places new demands on the adolescent which cannot be met with childhood behaviors and fantasies.

From adolescence through young adulthood the primary tasks confronting us are the preparation for a vocation and for assuming adult responsibilities. The focus is on education, beginning a career, getting married, and starting a family. Energy is directed outward, away from the self, and the attitude during these years is usually extraversion. The conscious is dominant and the goal of life is to achieve, to make a place in the world. For those who are successful, young adulthood is a challenging time of life, a succession of new vistas, horizons, and accomplishments. The young adult is enthusiastic and zestful about the excitement of life.

But then *middle age* strikes around age forty, causing depressing and radical changes in the personality. It might seem that middle age should be a period of immense satisfaction with the reasonably good adjustments most of us make to the demands of life. We are usually well established in our careers, communities, and families, and often financially secure. For many of us the years of driving and striving have paid off and we can begin to relax and enjoy life.

This was precisely Jung's situation when he underwent his terrible ordeal, and two-thirds of his patients were at the same stage of life. What goes wrong during this midpoint of life? Why, when success has finally been achieved, are we gripped by despair, misery, and feelings of worthlessness? Jung listened to his patients and they told him essentially the same thing in case after case: adventure, excitement, and zest had gone out of life. Life had lost its meaning; they felt empty and deadened.

The more Jung analyzed this period of life (his own and his patients'), the more he came to believe that such drastic changes in the personality at this time of life are inevitable and universal. Middle age is a natural time of transition in which the personality is undergoing necessary and beneficial changes.

The reason for this change, Jung found, lies, ironically, in the fact that middle-aged persons have been successful in meeting life's demands. Great energy had been invested in the preparatory activities of the first half of life but by age forty the preparation is finished, the challenges have been met. Yet the person still possesses great energy, but now it has nowhere to go. It must be reinvested in a different facet of life.

Jung noted that the first half of life focused on the external world. The second half of life must be devoted to the inner, subjective world which heretofore had been neglected. The attitude of the personality must become introversion. The previous focus on consciousness must be tempered by an awareness of unconscious experiences. The person's interests must shift from the physical and material to the religious, philosophical, and intuitive, and the previous one-sidedness (the focus on consciousness) must be replaced by a greater balance among all facets of the personality in order to begin the process of achieving self-realization.

The person in middle age cannot continue to be guided by the values of youth—seeking money, prestige, fame, or position. These have lost meaning. A new meaning must be found. If not, the person is condemned to a bankruptcy of the spirit and unspeakable despair.

Jung believed that this attempt to find meaning has become increasingly difficult due to the erosion of religion as a value in our lives. However, there is no escaping the need for new values, a fresh orientation, and a new way of looking at life. Those who are successful in integrating harmoniously the unconscious with the conscious, and in experiencing their own inner beings, are in a position to achieve positive psychological health, the condition Jung called *individuation*.

The final stage of personality growth is *old age*. Jung wrote little about old age but he did note a similarity between the last years of life and the first. In both old age and childhood the unconscious is dominant; the personality is totally submerged in it. Elderly persons must not look backwards. They need a goal to orient them toward the future. Again, the decline of religious values has been harmful, for fewer people cling to the promise (the goal) of life after death. Yet the inevitability of death must somehow be looked upon as a goal in itself, as something toward which we can strive. Our psychological health depends on it.

THE INDIVIDUATED PERSON

Let us discuss more fully Jung's version of the healthy personality. We have mentioned some of the requisites for psychological health. Our task is to bring those conceptions together to form a unified whole; this is, in essence, how the process of individuation works.

The first requirement of individuation is that the person be aware of those aspects of the self which have been neglected. This cannot occur until middle age. Jung defined the individuation process as that of becoming a unique individual, a single, homogeneous being. "It also implies becoming one's own self. We could therefore translate individuation as 'coming to selfhood' or 'self-realization.' "[9]

Individuation is instinctive, a goal to be striven for but rarely reached. (Jung gave as examples of fully individuated personalities Jesus Christ and Buddha.) To strive toward individuation we must give up the behaviors, values, and thoughts that guided the first half of life and reach into our unconscious. We must confront the unconscious as Jung did, boldly, openly, without reservation or inhibition. We must bring the voice of the unconscious to our awareness, listening, accepting, and following what it tells us. We must attend to and heed our dreams and fantasies. We must exercise what Jung called "creative imagination" in painting, writing, or some other form of expression, letting our hand be guided not by conscious, rational thought but by the spontaneous flow of the unconscious. The unconscious reveals our true selves to us.

However, admitting these unconscious forces into our lives does not mean becoming dominated by them. It means allowing them

9. C. G. Jung, *Two Essays on Analytical Psychology* (New York: Pantheon, 1953), p. 171. (Bollingen Series xx, Collected Works of C. G. Jung, Vol. 7.)

expression and assimilating them with the conscious processes. Thus, conscious and unconscious forces become equal partners.

There is no dominance of any one facet of personality in the individuated person, not by consciousness or unconsciousness, by a specific function or attitude, or by any of the archetypes. They are all brought into a harmonious balance.

Does this diminished emphasis on the conscious side of personality mean that a healthy person's life is less guided by rational factors? Yes, that seems to be true and it is necessary, according to Jung. To live solely in accordance with rational principles is to stunt our full humanness. "We should never identify ourselves with reason," Jung wrote, "for man is not and never will be a creature of reason alone."[10] Unconscious, irrational forces are too important a part of human nature to continue to be ignored (as they are during the first half of life when one is striving for success).

The second aspect of individuation involves the sacrifice of the material goals of young adulthood and the personality characteristics that enabled one to achieve those goals. The goals of the first half of life are meaningless for the second half and so are the attitudes and functions of that period. Recall that one attitude (extraversion or introversion) and one function (sensing, intuiting, thinking, or feeling) are dominant in young adulthood; all others are subordinated. This one-sidedness of personality so necessary in the first half of life becomes totally inappropriate during the second.

In individuation, no single function or attitude is dominant; they are all capable of being expressed and indeed must all be expressed. These aspects of the personality must be brought into balance.

For example, if you were an extravert in your twenties you would, in midlife, have to become conscious of your qualities of introversion as well. If your behavior had been dominated by the thinking function, you would also have to become conscious of your sensing, intuiting, and feeling functions. All of the formerly opposing characteristics and qualities must now be given expression.

Jung referred to the dominance of one attitude and function as a psychological *type*. The types form the major dimension which distinguishes one person from another. With individuation, paradoxically, these categories of individual difference disappear because the person can no longer be categorized as, say, a thinking extravert or a feeling introvert. Thus, there is much similarity among individuated persons.

10. Ibid., p. 71.

Another change in the personality in middle age involves shifts in the nature of the archetypes. Changes occur in the persona, shadow, and anima/animus during individuation. In fact, these changes are required for individuation to take place.

The first change is the dissolving or dethronement of the persona. The masks we wear, the social roles we play, must be continued throughout middle age—we still have to get along with many different people. However, although we may wear a public personality, we recognize that it may not represent our true nature. We must get beneath our persona and come to grips with the genuine self the persona has been covering. In other words, we must become ourselves.

Next, as individuated persons we must become aware of all the forces of the shadow, destructive and constructive. We must understand and accept the dark side of our nature, our animalistic, primitive impulses such as destructiveness and selfishness. This does not mean giving in to them or being dominated by them, but simply acceptance of their existence.

With the help of the persona in the first half of life we concealed this dark side of ourselves. We wanted others to know only our good side. So effectively did we conceal the shadow from others that we also concealed it from ourselves. This must change if individuation is to take place successfully. It is part of the process of self-knowledge, without which self-realization is impossible. Also, a greater awareness of the shadow can give a deeper dimension to our personality because it is the shadow's animalistic tendencies that bring zest, spontaneity, and vitality to our lives.

Once again we are bringing one facet of personality into a greater harmony with the others. Awareness of only the good side of our natures produces a one-sided development of personality. As with all the other opposing components of personality, both sides of this dimension must be allowed expression before individuation can be achieved.

Next in the individuation process is the necessity of coming to terms with our psychological bisexuality. A man must come to express his anima (feminine) traits and a woman must come to express her animus (masculine) traits. Every step in the individuation process is difficult, but the recognition in oneself of qualities and characteristics of the other sex is clearly the hardest. It represents the greatest change, the sharpest departure from the previous self-image.

Both sides of our nature must be expressed, achieving a balance to replace the exclusive dominance of one part over the other. Accepting our bisexual nature opens new sources of creativity that we never suspected (or admitted) we had and also serves as the final release from childhood influences. Jung wrote that it is not until the anima and animus are freely expressed that men are finally freed from their mothers and women freed from their fathers.

Jung has not presented us with a list of the characteristics of the healthy personality as other theorists have done. He did not draw a detailed portrait of such a person. However, scattered through his writings are enough images which, if drawn together, provide if not a photograph at least an impressionistic painting of the individuated person. Note that I have inferred these characteristics from Jung's system; they were not explicitly stated by him.

Individuated persons are in the middle years or older and have weathered the severe crises that result from the changing nature of personality during that time. They may have spent several years in contemplation of their selves, lives, ambitions, hopes, and goals. They have allowed their unconscious to be manifested so that they are aware of the previously suppressed side of their nature. As a result, individuated persons have achieved a high level of *self-knowledge;* they know themselves at both conscious and unconscious levels.

Along with self-knowledge comes *acceptance of self.* Individuated persons accept what their period of self-exploration has revealed to them. They accept their own nature—its strengths and weaknesses, the saintly side and the demonic side. While they may wear different personas in different situations, it is only a matter of social convenience. Individuated persons know they are playing roles but they do not confuse these roles with their true selves.

A third characteristic of individuated persons is *integration of self.* All aspects of the personality are integrated and harmonized so that all can be expressed—the opposite sex characteristics, the previously nondominant attitude and functions, the whole body of the unconscious. For the first time in life no aspect, attitude, or function is dominant.

So central a part of psychological health is this integration and expression of all parts of the personality that we should consider *self-expression* a fourth characteristic of individuated persons.

Such persons could also be characterized by an *acceptance and tolerance of human nature* in general. Because they are so open to the collective unconscious (the repository of all the experiences of humankind), individuated persons have a greater awareness and tolerance of the human condition. This presumably provides them with a greater insight into the behavior of others because they recognize forces from our human heritage which influence all of us. For this reason, healthy persons may feel more empathy with humanity.

Healthy persons are characterized by an *acceptance of the unknown and mysterious,* as Jung was in his own life. Since they are no longer solely creatures of reason, they can admit into consciousness unconscious, irrational factors. They pay heed to dreams and fantasies and, while not abandoning the use of reason and logic, they temper those conscious processes with the forces of the unconscious. This acceptance of the unknown and mysterious may also include supernatural and spiritual phenomena ranging from a belief in clairvoyance to a belief in God.

Healthy persons have what Jung called a *universal personality.* Since no single aspect of the personality (an attitude, function, or any side of an archetype) is dominant any longer, the uniqueness of the individual disappears. Such persons can no longer be described as belonging to a particular psychological type. The man who at twenty-five may have been extremely masculine and extraverted and who functioned in the feeling mode, loses these specific qualities once individuation takes place. These qualities are no longer dominant, making it impossible to classify him as a particular psychological type.

A PERSONAL COMMENT

Jung's theory is unlike any other theory of the healthy personality. It stands apart and seems out of step with the twentieth-century emphasis on the conscious factors of reason and logic. It is controversial and seems to critics to be a confusing blend of the occult, the supernatural, and the religious. Yet it has been warmly received by many others. In general, Jung's work has been better accepted in the fields of religion, history, art, and literature than in psychology and psychiatry.

Jung did write of a human condition which many believe is characteristic of late twentieth-century existence: the lack of meaning in life and the absence of roots or connection with the past or with nature. Many agree that we have placed too much emphasis on reason and science and lost sight of broader spiritual and philosophical values.

Jung's position in this regard is moderate, not extreme. He did not advocate the abandonment of reason or a surrender to the control of the unconscious. We must exercise reason but it should be tempered with a greater awareness of our unconscious forces. Equality and unity of these opposing aspects of our being are the key.

Let us discuss specific issues. Jung's concepts of introversion and extraversion have been widely accepted. It is argued, however, that they are overly broad and simple classifications of conscious orientations. Indeed, as noted, Jung realized this and introduced the functions of thinking, feeling, sensing, and intuiting to describe more fully one's perceptions of and reactions to the world. That the combination of functions and attitudes in eight psychological types is sufficient to encompass the diversity of human behavior is, I think, questionable. The psychological types may apply only in a general sense (and perhaps this is all any theory can strive for legitimately).

Jung's notion of the collective unconscious is difficult for most people to accept. It seems clear to me that we are influenced by the accumulation of personal experiences that we store in the personal unconscious. After all, what is learning but a change introduced by exposure to the experiences and stimuli we have met and coped with in the past? While we do not consciously remember all these experiences, it is hard to deny their existence and influence on behavior. Psychoanalysts, and others who probe the human personality, have offered much evidence that our nature can be influenced by experiences which were once conscious but are no longer so.

However, the reality of the collective unconscious is less clear to me. I find it difficult to believe that "memories" from our primitive (even animal) ancestors predispose us to think and behave as humans have always thought and behaved. The notion is intellectually and emotionally intriguing—it excites my interest and curiosity—but I view it with a good deal of skepticism. We can see that the evolution of the human race has been characterized by certain common, universal experiences. Human beings in every age share birth and death, a mother figure, or some sort of god. But have these experiences, as Jung suggested, been continuously transmitted to each new generation?

Jung found common themes and symbols in his fantasies and dreams and in those of his patients. He found them as well in different cultures and eras. This testifies to the universality of the experiences but it is not conclusive evidence that they have been inherited in some form. It may indicate only that human beings in every age are exposed to similar experiences and react similarly, for any number of reasons.

One aspect of Jung's theory which I do find congenial is his recognition of the important changes in personality which take place in middle age. In my counseling work with men and women in middle age I see the same stresses and strains Jung described. These individuals complain of staleness and meaninglessness in life and they long for the zest, enthusiasm, and excitement they knew in the years of early adulthood.

The growing psychological literature on the midlife transition supports Jung's notion that it is a period of universal and inevitable personality change. It is a time when persons begin to turn inward to their subjective being and look for new values and meanings to replace those no longer appropriate.

Jung's discussion of the nature of the healthy personality is not as clear-cut as that of other theorists. It is more difficult with Jung to envision precisely what healthy persons are like. I would like to know more about the specific characteristics such persons possess. It is clear that they know and accept themselves, that they accept and tolerate others, that they have integrated selves and universal personalities. But beyond these general and somewhat vague characteristics there is much we do not know about them. Other theorists have given us more finely drawn portraits of the healthy personality.

Jung was quite explicit that his concept of psychological health applies to only a chosen few. Realization of the self is reserved for bright, well-educated persons who have sufficient leisure time for a successful confrontation with the unconscious. (Jung's patients were all in this category.) The overwhelming majority of people, then, seem doomed to miss this supreme state of development.

Whatever the ultimate disposition of or judgment upon Jung's theory, it is certainly one of the more provocative and challenging ever offered. While his works are not easy to read, they do reveal a man of phenomenal genius who possessed an overwhelming sense of history and a profound respect for the hidden side of the human personality. Whether Jung's insights are revealing of human nature in general or only of his own nature remains to be seen. In the meantime, he has left us with intriguing forms and shapes to try to fit into the puzzle of the human personality.

BIBLIOGRAPHY

Bennet, E. A. *What Jung Really Said.* New York: Schocken Books, 1967.

Fordham, M., ed. *Contact with Jung.* Philadelphia: Lippincott, 1963.

Frey-Rohn, L. *From Freud to Jung.* New York: Putnam, 1974.

Jaffe, A. *The Myth of Meaning.* New York: Putnam, 1971.

Jung, C. G. *Modern Man in Search of a Soul.* New York: Harcourt, Brace, 1933.

——. *Two Essays on Analytical Psychology.* New York: Pantheon, 1953. (Bollingen Series xx, Collected Works of C. G. Jung, Vol. 7.)

——. *The Development of Personality.* New York: Pantheon, 1954. (Collected Works, Vol. 17.)

——. *Memories, Dreams, Reflections.* New York: Vintage Books, 1961.

Jung, C. G., ed. *Man and His Symbols.* New York: Dell, 1968.

7

The self-transcendent person
Frankl's model

At the age of thirty-seven, Viktor Frankl (1905–) began a three-year odyssey into a nightmare world of human cruelty, torture, starvation, and privation from which death seemed the only escape. His descent into hell began on a train from his native Vienna, Austria, and moved in a northeasterly direction. None of the 1500 passengers knew where they were going. There were eighty people in Frankl's coach. It was so crowded that they had to sleep on their luggage and the personal possessions they carried with them.

For several days and nights the train sped through cities and open countryside. Finally one early morning it slowed and was shunted onto a spur. The passengers looked anxiously through the windows, desperate to learn where they were. Then the name of the station came into view; a few cried out but most were grimly silent. The sign read "Auschwitz."

Gradually, as dawn broke, the barbed wire and watch towers of the most infamous Nazi death camp came into view. In his imagination Frankl saw rows of gallows with corpses dangling on them. "I was horrified, but this was just as well, because step by step, we had to become accustomed to a terrible and immense horror."[1]

The year was 1942 and Viktor Frankl entered the world of organized, efficient murder that was to claim the lives of six million of his fellow Jews. He would be one of the few—the very few—who would survive. But his body and mind endured suffering that words

1.   V. Frankl, *Man's Search for Meaning* (New York: Simon and Schuster, 1962), p. 7.

cannot fully describe, a crucible which, in the end, provided the severest test of all he had ever believed in. His father, mother, brother, wife—every member of the family except a sister—were killed in the holocaust. Yet he survived. But more than that, Frankl endured this ordeal strengthened by a belief in the human capacity to find meaning and purpose in life in the face of overwhelming suffering, even on the threshold of death.

In the preface of Frankl's book *Man's Search for Meaning*, Gordon Allport wrote: "How could he—every possession lost, every value destroyed, suffering from hunger, cold and brutality, hourly expecting extermination—how could he find life worth preserving? A psychiatrist who personally has faced such extremity is a psychiatrist worth listening to."[2]

The train doors were flung open and the passengers ordered outside on the platform. Harsh, gutteral commands were shouted at them and they were formed into two lines, women in one and men in the other. Slowly the long lines of prisoners moved forward to pass in front of an elegantly uniformed SS officer. The man glanced briefly at each person and then casually pointed a finger to the right or to the left. No one knew what it meant at first but as the lines shortened they could see that most of them were being sent to the left.

When it was Frankl's turn the SS man stared at him for a longer time than he had at any of the others. Then the Nazi reached out and placed both hands on Frankl's shoulder and turned him very slowly to the right. Later that evening, Frankl asked a prisoner who had been in the camp for some time where a friend, who had been sent to the left side, was. "You can see him there," the man replied, and he pointed to a tall chimney spewing flame and smoke. Ninety percent of Frankl's fellow passengers—more than 1300 persons—had been killed before noon.

The remaining prisoners were required to surrender all their possessions—clothes, jewelry, notebooks. Frankl was carrying the manuscript of what was to have been his first book; he desperately wanted to keep it. That sheaf of papers contained his life's work. Hurriedly and furtively he explained the importance of this work to an old prisoner. The man began to grin—a mocking, sneering, insulting grin—and when he spoke it was only to say "Shit!" "At that moment I saw the plain truth and did what marked the culminating point of the

2. Ibid., p. ix.

first phase of my psychological reaction: I struck out my whole former life."[3,4]

The manuscript was Frankl's spiritual child and he was faced with the decision whether life held any meaning in the face of that tragic loss. The question was answered for him within the hour. In the pocket of the clothing of a dead prisoner he was given to wear he found a scrap of paper torn from a Hebrew prayer book. It contained the prayer *Shema Yisrael:* "Love thy God with all thy heart, and with all thy soul, and with all thy might." Frankl interpreted this differently from the orthodox religious meaning. To him it became "the command to say yes to life despite whatever one has to face, be it suffering or even dying."[5]

Frankl decided that if the value and meaning of his life rested solely on whether a manuscript would be published, then life was not really worth living. Surely there must be a greater meaning to life. And for Frankl at that time, in that place, the single scrap of paper became more valuable than his lost work. The prayer was a "symbolic call" to live the philosophy he developed, to test it in the harsh laboratory of the concentration camp, not merely putting it on paper. The main ideas of his theory had been developed before Auschwitz but they were empirically validated by his experiences there. Indeed, this may have enabled him to survive.

From 1942 until 1945, Viktor Frankl, M.D., neurologist, psychiatrist, former head of the neurology department of the Rothschild Hospital in Vienna, was number 119,104, first in Auschwitz and then in Dachau. Most of that time was spent digging ditches and tunnels or laying railroad tracks, often in sub-freezing weather with only the flimsiest clothing for protection. Later he wrote movingly of the horrors he experienced and the lessons he learned from the realization that he had "nothing to lose except his so ridiculously naked life."[6]

Frankl returned from the camps with the knowledge born of first-hand experience that human beings have, in any and all situations, a choice over their actions. We are able to preserve, even in the darkest moments, some remnant of spiritual freedom, a fragment of

---

3. Ibid., p. 12.
4. In his three years of imprisonment, Frankl wrote down key words and phrases of the manuscript from memory on tiny scraps of paper and in 1955 the book was published: *The Doctor and the Soul: An Introduction to Logotherapy* (New York: Knopf).
5. From V. Frankl, "Address before the Third Annual Meeting of the Academy of Religion and Mental Health, 1962," reprinted in F. T. Severin, *Discovering Man in Psychology* (New York: McGraw-Hill, 1973), p. 134.
6. V. Frankl, *Man's Search for Meaning* (New York: Simon and Schuster, 1962), pp. x–xi.

independence. He learned that human beings can lose everything they value except the most fundamental human freedom: the freedom to choose an attitude or way of reacting to our fate, the freedom to choose our own way.

We can retain the ultimate power to decide the outcome of our existence. This element of spiritual freedom cannot be taken from us; it gives life meaning and purpose and without it there is no reason for surviving. Frankl quoted Nietzsche on this point of view: "He who has a *why* to live can bear with almost any *how*."[7]

What matters in human existence is not so much the fate that awaits us but the way in which we accept that fate. And Frankl believed that meaning can be found in all circumstances, including suffering and death. To be alive is to suffer, he wrote, but to find some meaning in one's suffering is to survive.

When the war ended, Frankl returned to Vienna as the head of the neurology department of the Poliklinic Hospital and professor of neurology and psychiatry at the University of Vienna Medical School. He resumed his work on the importance for human existence of the will to meaning, a system he called *logotherapy*.

In the years since then, Frankl has persistently and diligently refined and disseminated his view of human nature through articles, lectures, and seventeen books, many of which have been translated into several languages. He has made more than thirty visits to the United States and has taught at Harvard and Southern Methodist universities. From 1970 to 1973 he was a professor at the U.S. International University in San Diego where he now spends a portion of each year.

Frankl's logotherapy has a wide following among psychologists, psychiatrists, and others. Many feel that his work is particularly relevant to the problems of our time and culture.

FRANKL'S APPROACH TO PERSONALITY

Frankl's view of psychological health stresses the importance of the *will to meaning*. Indeed, this is the framework within which everything else is organized. First, however, let us deal with the name he has given his system: logotherapy. The word "logos," taken from the Greek, translates as "meaning." Logotherapy, then, deals with the meaning of human existence and the human need for meaning, as

7. Ibid., p. 76.

well as with specific therapeutic techniques for finding meaning in life.[8]

As such, logotherapy is primarily a method of psychotherapy for dealing with persons whose lives lack meaning. It is more technique than theory. However, as Frankl points out, there cannot be a form of psychotherapy which is not based on a theory of human nature and a philosophy of life. (As with other theorists, we shall focus here only on the theory of personality, not on the techniques devised by the theorist to change personality.)

The theory of human nature which derives from logotherapy is built on three pillars: the freedom of will, the will to meaning, and the meaning of life. Frankl strongly opposes those positions in psychology and psychiatry which characterize the human condition as determined by biological instincts or childhood conflicts or any other external force. He argues that while we are subject to external conditions which affect our lives (as happened to him in Auschwitz), we are nevertheless free to choose our reaction to these conditions. We are not impervious to outside forces—they can and do change our circumstances—but we are free to take our own stand in dealing with them. This gives us the ultimate freedom to rise above circumstances and fate.

The other pillars—the will to meaning and the meaning of life— refer to our continuing need to search not for our selves but for a meaning to supply a purpose for our existence. The more we are able to transcend ourselves—to give ourselves to a cause or to a person— the more fully human we become. This becomes the ultimate criterion for the development of a healthy personality: our immersion in some person or thing beyond ourselves. Only in this way can we truly become ourselves.

Our search for meaning involves *personal responsibility*. No one and nothing else—not parents, spouse, or nation—can supply us with a sense of meaning and purpose in our lives. It is our responsibility to find our own way and to persist in it once found. We must, as Frankl did himself, responsibly and freely confront the conditions of our existence and find in them a purpose. Life constantly challenges us and our response must be not in talk or contemplation but in deeds, giving overt expression to the meaning we find in our lives.

The lack of meaning in life is, to Frankl, a neurosis; he calls this

8. In the 1930s Frankl called his approach *Existenzanalyse* (existential analysis). However, the term "existential analysis" has since been used in this country quite loosely to refer to several theorists, including Frankl. To avoid this confusion, Frankl now uses only "logotherapy" to describe his system.

condition *noögenic neurosis.*[9] This is a state characterized by meaning-lessness, purposelessness, aimlessness, and emptiness. Frankl wrote about his fellow prisoners: "Woe to him who saw no more sense in his life, no aim, no purpose, and therefore no point in carrying on. He was soon lost."[10] Instead of feeling full and vibrant with life, such a person exists in an *existential vacuum,* a condition Frankl believes is common in our modern age.

Many of us suffer the boredom and apathy of noögenic neurosis as a consequence of two conditions. First, when humans evolved from lower animals, they lost the natural drives and instincts that connected them with nature. While this has freed us from certain constraints, it means that we are not instinctively guided in our behavior; we must actively choose what to do.

Second, in the late twentieth century we have few conventions, traditions, and values to prescribe our behavior. As the forces of or-ganized religion and social convention wane, we are left even more on our own, confronted with making our own decisions and taking responsibility for them.

Frankl finds evidence of an existential vacuum on a large scale in many cultures, both capitalist and communist, and he believes that it is spreading rapidly, particularly in the United States. Frankl's solu-tion to widespread noögenic neurosis is for each of us to find or regain the vital sense of meaning and purpose in life. Otherwise we are doomed to psychological ill-health.

Logotherapy proposes three ways by which we can give meaning to life: (1) by what we give to the world in terms of some creation, (2) by what we take from the world in experience, and (3) by the attitude we take toward suffering.

THE NATURE OF HEALTHY HUMAN EXISTENCE

Frankl believes that three factors comprise the essence of human existence: spirituality, freedom, and responsibility.

Spirituality is a difficult concept to define. It is irreducible. It can-not be explained in material terms. While it can be affected by the ma-

---

9. Frankl coined the term "noögenic neurosis" to distinguish this condition from the usual neuroses which derive from some psychological conflict within the individual. "Noos" in Greek means "mind." Thus, noögenic neurosis pertains to the spiritual core of personality, not in a religious sense but as a dimension of human exis-tence. Specifically, noögenic neurosis refers to moral conflicts.
10. V. Frankl, *Man's Search for Meaning* (New York: Simon and Schuster, 1962), p. 76.

terial world, it is not caused or produced by that world. Perhaps we can best think of it as the spirit or the soul.

We have already noted the importance of *freedom* in Frankl's system. We are not dictated to by nonspiritual factors—by instinct, our specific inheritance, or the conditions of our environment. We have and must use our freedom to choose how we will behave if we are to be psychologically healthy. Those who do not experience this freedom are either prejudiced by a belief in determinism or severely neurotic (in the traditional, not noögenic, sense). Neurotics block the fulfillment of their own potentialities, thus interfering with their full human development.

Finally, it is not enough to feel free to choose, we must also accept the *responsibility* of choosing. Logotherapy reminds us of our responsibility in this way: "Live as if you were living for the second time and had acted as wrongly the first time as you are about to act now."[11] Frankl believes that if we confront ourselves in this situation we will become instantly aware of the grave responsibility we have for every hour of every day.

Healthy persons will bear this responsibility, despite the brief and transitory nature of life, using their time wisely lest their work (their lives) remain undeveloped. If we die before we finish sculpting the form of our lives, what we have done is not negated. The meaningfulness of a life is judged by its quality, not its longevity. It is less important that the work of life be finished than that it be begun and continued on a high level. "Sometimes the 'unfinisheds' are among the most beautiful symphonies."[12]

Spirituality, freedom, and responsibility—these are up to us to attain and use. Without them it is impossible to find meaning and purpose in life. The choices are literally ours alone to make.

THE MOTIVATION OF THE HEALTHY PERSONALITY

In Frankl's system there is one fundamental motivation, the *will to meaning*, which is so powerful that it is capable of overshadowing all other human motivations. It is vital for psychological health and, in extreme situations (such as Frankl faced in Auschwitz), it is necessary for sheer survival. Without meaning to life there is no reason to continue living.

11. V. Frankl, *The Doctor and the Soul: From Psychotherapy to Logotherapy*, 2nd ed. (New York: Knopf, 1965), p. 64.
12. Ibid., p. 66.

The meaning of life is inevitably idiosyncratic, unique to each individual. It differs from person to person and even from one moment to the next. There is no such thing as a universal will to meaning, one which applies in a general way to all human beings.

Just as the tasks of an individual's life are real, so too is the meaning of life. The tasks we set for ourselves form our destiny and it cannot be compared with anyone else's. Also, the situations in which we find ourselves—the circumstances under which we try to fulfill our tasks—are never repeated. We cannot encounter the same situation twice in the same way because of the influence of new experiences that have occurred in the period between the two situations.

Since tasks and destinies are unique to individuals and time periods, each person must find his or her own way of responding. Similarly, we must find the meaning of life that is appropriate for each of us. And when we are confronted with a different situation, we may have to find a different meaning to give to life, as Frankl did when his situation changed from that of a secure, respected physician to number 119,104 in Auschwitz. Some situations require us to actively shape our fate, others to accept it, to bear a cross. Each situation is new and requires a separate response.

Despite the variation in what gives meaning to life, Frankl insisted that there was only one answer to each situation. The problem for us is not that some situations have no meaning—they all do have meaning—but how to find that meaning.

The search for meaning, then, can be a perplexing and challenging task, and one which increases not decreases inner tension. In fact, Frankl sees this tension increase as a prerequisite for psychological health. A life devoid of tension, a life oriented toward stability and equilibrium of internal tension, is doomed to noögenic neurosis; this life lacks meaning. A healthy personality contains a certain level of tension between what has been achieved or accomplished and what ought to be achieved or accomplished, a gap between what we are and what we should become.

This gap means that healthy persons are always striving for goals that supply a meaning to life. These persons are continually faced with the challenge of finding new purposes to fulfill. And this continuing struggle provides zest and excitement to life. The alternative—abandoning the search—creates an existential vacuum and makes us feel bored, apathetic, and purposeless. Life has no meaning; we have no reason to continue living.

We noted earlier three ways in which we can give meaning to life: what we give to the world in terms of some creation, what we take from the world in experience, and the attitude we take toward suffering. Frankl discusses these under the general heading *values*. Values, like the meaning of life to which they lead, are unique to each person and situation. They are variable and flexible in order to adapt to the diverse circumstances in which we find ourselves. Throughout our lives we must constantly address ourselves to the problem of values, perpetually choosing the one which gives meaning to life in each situation.

There are three fundamental systems of values, corresponding to the three ways of giving meaning to life: creative values, experiential values, and attitudinal values.

Creative values are realized in creative and productive activity. Usually this refers to some kind of work, although creative values can be expressed in all areas of life. Meaning is given to life through the act of creating a tangible product or an intangible idea or by serving others, which is an expression of the individual.

While creative values involve giving to the world, *experiential values* involve receiving from the world. This receptivity can provide as much meaning as creativity. Experiential values are manifested by surrendering oneself to beauty in the worlds of nature or art. Frankl argues that it is possible to fulfill life's meaning by the intensity with which some aspects of life are experienced, independent of any positive action taken by the individual.

Frankl offers the example of a music lover listening to the performance of a favorite symphony. At that moment, the person is intensely involved with a pure form of beauty. Suppose we asked that person whether life had any meaning. Frankl believes that the person "would have to reply that it had been worthwhile living if only to experience this ecstatic moment. For even though only a single moment is in question—the greatness of a life can be measured by the greatness of a moment."[13]

With that example, Frankl introduces another aspect to the meaning of life: meaning may exist at only certain times. In other words, we may not find meaning in all moments of existence. However, the fact that meaning may occur only sporadically does not detract from the overall meaningfulness of life. Just as the height of a mountain range is not described by the level of the valleys, Frankl wrote, but by the highest peak, so do we describe the meaningfulness of a life by its peaks, not its valleys. He argued that even a single peak moment of experiential value can fill a person's entire life with mean-

13. Ibid., pp. 43–44.

ing. The deciding factor seems to be not how many peaks we reach or how long we stay at such a level, but rather the intensity with which we experience the ones we do have.

Creative and experiential values deal with rich, full, positive human experiences, a fullness of life through either creating or experiencing. But life is not composed solely of ennobling and enriching experiences. Other forces and events constrain our lives: illness, death, or the kind of situation Frankl faced in Auschwitz. How may we find meaning under such negative conditions when there is neither beauty to experience nor the opportunity to express creativity?

This is where the third set of values—*attitudinal values*—comes into play. Frankl believes that it is not so much our objective fate that is so dispiriting and destructive as the attitudes we hold toward our fate. It is the most abysmal, despairing, and seemingly hopeless situations that Frankl sees as providing us with the greatest opportunity for finding meaning. And they are also the situations that most strongly demand that a meaning be found.

The situations which call forth attitudinal values are those we are powerless to change or avoid—unalterable conditions of fate. When we are confronted by such a situation, the only rational way of responding is acceptance. The way in which we accept our fate, the courage with which we bear our suffering, the dignity we display in the face of disaster, is the ultimate test and measure of our fulfillment as human beings.

By incorporating attitudinal values as a way of giving meaning to life, Frankl gives us hope that human existence, even in extreme circumstances, can be characterized by meaning and purpose. Our lives can retain meaning up to the final moment of existence. As long as we are conscious, we are obligated to realize values. It is a human responsibility we must not evade if we are to maintain psychological health.

Those who find meaning in life reach the state of *self-transcendence,* the ultimate state of being for the healthy personality.

THE NATURE OF THE SELF-TRANSCENDENT PERSON

In Frankl's view, our major motivation in life is to search not for self but for meaning; this involves, in a sense, "forgetting" ourselves. The psychologically healthy person has moved beyond or transcended the focus on self. Being fully human means relating to someone or something beyond one's self. Frankl compared this quality of self-transcendence with the ability of the human eye to see the world outside itself which is directly related to the eye's inability to see anything within itself. In fact, in situations where the eye does see itself—for example, when it is covered by a cataract which becomes the only thing it can see—it is unable to see anything beyond itself. Sight, then, is self-transcendent; it must deal only with something beyond itself in order for it to function.

This view puts Frankl's position in opposition to theorists who argue that the goal or motivation of full human development is the fulfillment or actualization of the self. Frankl denies human striving to establish any state or condition within the self, whether for power, pleasure, or actualization. Such a view, he argues, depicts the person as a closed system concerned not with interaction with the real world or with other persons but only with the self. The pursuit of a goal exclusively within the self is, Frankl believes, self-defeating.

Let us examine two self-oriented goals: pleasure and self-actualization. Frankl states that the more we deliberately strive for pleasure, the less likely we are to find it. A life oriented toward the pursuit of happiness will never find happiness. The more we focus on happiness as a goal, the more we will lose sight of the reason for being happy. Frankl offers the example of persons who focus on sexual pleasure. He estimates, based on his own work with patients, that more than 95 percent of impotence and frigidity cases result from the male's deliberate striving to demonstrate potency and the female's deliberate striving to demonstrate the capacity for orgasm. Such persons are too actively pursuing happiness instead of letting it occur as a by-product of the search for meaning in life.

Pleasure and happiness do occur and add to the enjoyment of life, but they are not the goal of life. Happiness cannot be pursued and captured; it follows naturally and spontaneously from fulfilling meaning, from attaining a goal outside the self.

The same thing occurs, in principle, with the pursuit of self-actualization. The more we strive directly for self-actualization, the less likely we are to achieve it. Self-actualization is in opposition to self-transcendence and can be achieved only as a secondary effect of finding meaning in life. Thus, the only way to become self-actualizing is through fulfilling a meaning beyond the self.

Frankl believes that his views are compatible with Maslow's view that the best way to achieve self-actualization is through a commitment to work, to something beyond the self.[14] A focus solely on self-

14.   Maslow also wrote of the self being transcended during peak experiences.

actualization results from the frustration of the will to meaning. To illustrate this, Frankl uses the example of a boomerang. The purpose of the boomerang is not to return to the person who has thrown it; the boomerang returns only when it has missed its target.

Similarly, persons return to themselves (focus on themselves) when they have lost sight of their meaning and purpose in the world. When they have missed the target (their task and meaning) and thereby frustrated their will to meaning, they become intent only upon their selves. To be psychologically healthy is to move beyond the focus on self, to transcend it, to absorb it in one's meaning and purpose. Then the self will be spontaneously and naturally fulfilled and actualized.

Frankl does not present a list of characteristics of the healthy personality. However, we have already noted in general what such persons are like:

1. They are free to choose their own course of action.
2. They are personally responsible for the conduct of their lives and the attitude they hold toward their fate.
3. They are not determined by forces outside themselves.
4. They have found a meaning in life which suits them.
5. They are in conscious control of their lives.
6. They are able to manifest creative, experiential, or attitudinal values.
7. They have transcended the concern with self.

There are several other characteristics of healthy personalities. They are oriented toward the future, directed toward future goals and tasks. Indeed, they need such goals. "It is a peculiarity of man," Frankl wrote, "that he can only live by looking to the future."[15] Frankl observed many fellow prisoners in Auschwitz who lost their sense of future, who gave up their orientation toward specific goals, and they died within a few days. Without a belief in the future, the "spiritual hold" on life is lost, and the mind and body are doomed to rapid decay.

We must have a reason to continue living, a future goal to accomplish, or life loses its meaning. Frankl recounted a personal experience in this regard. He was in terrible pain, cold, hungry, and frightened. All seemed lost. But then he forced himself to think about something else and suddenly he had an image of himself in a warm

15. V. Frankl, *Man's Search for Meaning* (New York: Simon and Schuster, 1962), p. 72.

and attractive lecture hall speaking about the psychology of concentration camps. His oppressed spirit rose because he rose above his situation and transcended the suffering and despair of the moment.

Note that Frankl said he *forced* himself to think of other things. He stresses that we are free to choose how we react to our circumstances, a freedom that can never be taken from us.

Another characteristic of the self-transcendent person is the commitment to work. One way of achieving meaning is through the expression of creative values—giving something to the world—and these values can be best expressed through a person's vocation or mission. It is an aspect of life which places us in a unique relationship to society; we perform our work in a manner practiced by no other person and so we each make a contribution to society.

The important aspect of work is not the content of the job but the way in which we perform it. This is what gives meaning to life. Thus, what is important is not the job (the external force) but what we bring to the job in terms of our personality as unique human beings (the internal force). Frankl gave the example of a woman working as a nurse. She performs many necessary acts each day but those acts (the job's requirements) are not sufficient to provide her life with meaning. It is only when the nurse does something more, beyond what her duties command, that she finds meaning through her work. When she spends extra time to console a frightened patient or says a few kind words to someone near death, she is giving of herself beyond the structure of her work, focusing on someone beyond herself.

Since we find meaning *through* work, not *in* it, meaning can be found through almost any kind of work. Frankl believes that most jobs allow for the expression of creative values (except those that are totally regimented, such as an assembly line job).

Another characteristic of self-transcendent persons is their ability to give and receive love. Love is the ultimate human goal; our salvation is through love and in love. While one way to realize our uniqueness is through work, another is through being loved. When we are loved we are accepted by another person for our unique and singular being. We become, to the person who loves us, indispensable and irreplaceable.

But there is another side to a love relationship: giving love. By giving love to (being in love with) another person, we are able to see their distinctive traits and features, including those which have not yet been actualized. By our love, we can enable the loved one to realize those untapped potentials by making them aware of what they can become. In a reciprocated love relationship, both sides benefit in terms of great fulfillment and the realization of their potentiality to become more fully human.

A PERSONAL COMMENT

Frankl's system of logotherapy and his view of human nature have achieved a good deal of acceptance and recognition in Europe and the United States. Although not as well known as Freud's or Maslow's position, Frankl's work is slowly reaching a level of credibility that I think will ensure its continued growth and prominence.

I find Frankl's theory appealing for two reasons. First, there is the clarity and compassion with which his ideas are presented. In contrast to some other theorists, Frankl's books are delightful to read. This clearness of expression enables the reader to immediately understand the point being made, and the compassion makes the reader (at least this one) feel that Frankl is speaking from the depths of his own existence of human experiences which move us all. He does not present scientific evidence (not unlike other personality theorists), but because of the experiences he is describing and the manner in which he discusses them, I feel that Frankl is cutting sharply and cleanly to the essence of human existence.

Second, Frankl's point of view (like Jung's) was refined and tested by his own experience. To me, his writings have compelling face validity because he lived through those terrible events, came to grips with them, and resolved them successfully on the basis of his beliefs. Of course, we must recognize that the experiences of Frankl and Jung are not necessarily generalizable; it does not follow that everyone in those situations would be as successful in coping using the same beliefs and techniques. Yet Frankl and Jung later found additional support for their positions by testing them with large numbers of patients.

Let us examine specific points in Frankl's system. He addresses a problem that seems endemic to our time and place: the lack of meaning in our lives. This is a condition psychiatrists and psychologists are finding among their patients with increasing frequency. Growing numbers of us seem to have lost a "why" to live and this makes it more difficult to tolerate the "how" of our existence, however easy and affluent that existence may be.

The usefulness of Frankl's system is supported by the fact that it was applied under the extreme conditions of the Nazi concentration camps, far more extreme conditions than the most devious experimental psychologist could devise. If, through his belief in the will to meaning, Frankl could find a meaning in life under those circumstances, it does suggest that such an approach would be even more applicable under the conditions we face today. In other words, if his system was tested successfully under such harsh conditions, it seems that it should be even more useful under less harsh conditions. This, to me, is a point in its favor.

Frankl presents us with an optimistic picture of human nature. We are not conditioned robots responding only as we have been trained to respond. Nor are we the irreversible products of our toilet training or other childhood experiences. We are free of the past, not inhibited or constrained by it. Nor are we shaped exclusively by social and cultural forces; we are not blind followers of beliefs and mores. Finally, we are not dominated by the physical environment, no matter how oppressive it may be, nor by our own bodies, no matter how much suffering they may endure.

We are, Frankl tells us, free agents, able to choose how to behave and how to react to changing circumstances. We are independent of all forces and conditions save those which most forcefully compel us to give the added dimension of meaning and purpose to our lives. It is comforting to be told that we have the ultimate power within us to decide the outcome of our existence. We have a spiritual freedom which no outside force can negate. Whether this personal freedom is an innate dimension of human existence or a quality that we persuade ourselves we have, the outcome—in terms of freedom of choice—seems to be the same. If we believe something to be true, we act and feel and think in accordance with that belief; it becomes a self-fulfilling prophecy. Whatever its origin or reality, Frankl's spiritual freedom seems to be a necessary component not only of psychological health but of sheer survival.

Allied with this spiritual freedom as a dimension of human existence is the notion of personal responsibility. It is up to us to supply meaning and purpose to life; no one else can do it for us. How different from the deterministic philosophy which holds that we are not responsible for our actions, for the conduct of our lives. It is challenging (perhaps frightening) to know that what we make of life is our responsibility. But, in the long run—assuming one is capable and willing to accept that responsibility—it seems to be healthier and it may raise our view of what we can do and can become. Thus, the dimension of personal responsibility can lead to a greater fulfillment of human potentialities, to a much higher actualization of self (while recognizing that self-actualization is not the goal of life).

Frankl's discussion of the will to meaning seems somewhat vague to me, although its importance for psychological health is quite clear. And perhaps the concept must be discussed in general rather than specific terms since the will to meaning is highly idiosyncratic; in other words, we each must find our own meaning.

More specific are the three ways in which we can find meaning in life: the creative, experiential, and attitudinal values. We can find meaning actively, through work or some other creative activity, or passively, through experiencing beauty. And we can find meaning in the negative side of life, in suffering and death, through the attitude we deliberately choose to take toward our circumstances.

Frankl writes movingly of terminally ill patients who discover meaning in their misfortune and display great courage and dignity as a result. (Perhaps they also serve as inspiration to those who later experience suffering.) The current phrase "death with dignity" may refer to characteristics displayed by those who have found their will to meaning in the circumstances of their dying. This aspect of Frankl's system may offer the most hope for human beings. Since fewer of us find meaning in a belief in life after death, it is comforting to believe that we can find meaning in life in the preparation for death, in the act of dying.

The idea that psychological health involves a search not for self but for a meaning beyond the self is an interesting one which may be at odds with Maslow's point of view. (Although Maslow may have said the same thing in different terms; for example, his belief in the importance of work, of something beyond the self.) Frankl seems to suggest that too great a focus on the self ultimately inhibits psychological health. We must move beyond the self in order to achieve intimate and productive relationships with the world and with others.

As is the case with Jung's work, I find myself wanting to know more of the specific characteristics of Frankl's psychologically healthy persons, to have a more complete picture of what they are like. But we must be content with what Frankl has told us. We know that such persons are directed toward future goals, committed to meaning through their work and their love of (and by) others, responsible, freely choosing, and independent. We might certainly wish to possess these characteristics ourselves, or at least to believe we are capable of possessing them.

My overall reaction to Frankl's view of human nature is similar to my reaction to Maslow's view; I want to believe it. It seems to offer hope that life can be enriched and healthy, regardless of momentary circumstances. Frankl's prescription for psychological health contains no new or startling pronouncements, but what is persuasive is the hard forge of real world experience on which he tested his beliefs, the living laboratory in which they were applied and found useful. They obviously worked for him. Whether they will work for the rest of us is yet to be decided. But perhaps the real contribution of Frankl's system is the stress on the importance of believing in the existence of meaning, that meaning exists in every situation and that we are free and sufficiently responsible to find it.

BIBLIOGRAPHY

Frankl, V. *Man's Search for Meaning: An Introduction to Logotherapy.* Boston: Beacon Press, 1962.

——. *The Doctor and the Soul: From Psychotherapy to Logotherapy,* 2nd ed. New York: Knopf, 1965.

——. *The Will to Meaning: Foundations and Applications of Logotherapy.* Cleveland: World, 1969.

——. *The Unconscious God.* New York: Simon and Schuster, 1975.

Hall, M. A conversation with Viktor Frankl of Vienna. *Psychology Today,* 1968, 2, 57–63.

8

The "here and now" person
Perls' model

In 1936, Fritz Perls (1893–1970), a forty-three-year-old psychoanalyst, travelled 4000 miles from his home in South Africa to a long-anticipated meeting with Sigmund Freud. The occasion was the annual Psychoanalytic Congress, held that year in Czechoslovakia. Perls was excited about the trip and the paper he planned to present. He had written what he thought was a contribution, even an improvement, to psychoanalysis, and he was eager to see how his colleagues would accept it.

The affair turned out to be a humiliating disaster for Perls. The paper met with an unenthusiastic reception; his new ideas were not welcomed by the orthodox psychoanalytic society. Wilhelm Reich, who had once been Perls' analyst and had helped him a great deal, barely acknowledged his presence. But the greatest blow came from Freud himself.

Perls never got beyond the doorway of Freud's room. When he told Freud he had come all the way from South Africa to meet him, Freud replied, "Well, and when are you going back?"

Perls walked away crushed and shamefaced, feeling belittled and scorned. But shortly these feelings were replaced by anger. He left the Congress with one resolve: "I'll show you—you can't do this to me."[1]

---

1. The quotations in this chapter not otherwise attributed are from Frederick S. (Fritz) Perls' autobiography *In and Out of the Garbage Pail* (Lafayette, CA: Real People Press, 1969). The book is unpaged.

The meeting with Freud made a lasting impression on Perls.[2] His daughter noted that he returned from the Congress "a very different man." It brought about a total reorientation in his professional and personal life. He changed from a "mediocre psychoanalyst" (as he referred to himself) to a vigorous proponent of a new form of therapy and philosophy of human nature which he both preached for others and practiced in his own life. He became a living example of what he would urge others to become.

All of his previously repressed doubts and misgivings about psychoanalysis surfaced with a clarity that overwhelmed him. It was a time of awakening; he discarded his former beliefs and experienced a sudden freedom from the constraints that had guided him in the past. He decided that he didn't need support from any source outside himself. He would no longer depend on the spiritual, moral, or intellectual systems that he had used before. And he came to the realization that marks the essence of his Gestalt Therapy: "I had to take all responsibility for my existence myself."

Over the next several years Perls did just that. He withdrew from his professional identity as a Freudian psychoanalyst and from his close relationship with his family. Perls and his wife (also an analyst) had lived in luxury in Johannesburg, with servants, nursemaids, tennis courts, a swimming pool, even a private ice-skating rink. This was a far cry from their lives in 1935, penniless refugees from Germany living on charity in Holland. As South Africa's first psychoanalyst, Perls' practice was very successful and he surrounded himself with all the requisites of middle-class material success.

Upon his return from the disastrous trip to Czechoslovakia, he saw his success in a different light. "I was caught by all the trimmings of a square, respectable citizen: family, house, servants, making more money than I needed. I was caught in the dichotomy of work and play: Monday to Friday versus the weekend. I just extricated myself through my spite and rebelliousness."[3] Never would Perls be in such a situation again.

Although still living together, Perls and his wife went their separate ways as he strove to increase the emotional distance between himself and his family. He became brusque and irritable, carried on an affair (one of many during his lifetime) with the children's nurse,

2. Toward the end of his life, some thirty-four years later, Perls wrote that one of his "unfinished situations" was "to have a man-to-man encounter with Freud and to show him the mistakes he made."
3. This mood and theme would be echoed by a generation of American youth thirty years later.

involved himself in amateur films and plays, and developed his theory and therapy. He built his life and his theory around one basic idea, summed up by his "Gestalt prayer":

> I do my thing and you do your thing.
> I am not in this world to live up to your expectations
> And you are not in this world to live up to mine.
> You are you and I am I,
> And if by chance we find each other, it's beautiful.
> If not, it can't be helped.[4]

For the rest of his life—from South Africa to New York and Miami to the Esalen Institute in California—Perls did his own thing. He practiced what he preached and, in the process, became a therapist, guide, and inspiration to hundreds who knew him and to thousands who are following his prescription for living. He became a god to his followers and an irritating, crude, obnoxious, aging reprobate to those who were offended by his life style and his teachings.[5]

One thing his followers and detractors might agree on is that Perls was a colorful and eccentric individual. Whether conducting a workshop in Gestalt Therapy or lusting after a girl young enough to be his granddaughter (and usually succeeding), he did it with zest, passion, and a sense of joy that showed a genius for living what some would consider a full life.

Martin Shepard, a psychiatrist and follower of Gestalt Therapy, wrote a biography of Perls in 1975. He offers this description of the man: "He was, for me, a perfect animal—not in a low but in a high sense. He could be nasty or funny, crude or kind, lewd or loving, cheap or extravagant, *and he didn't bother to hide any of it.*"[6]

And of Perls in his seventies Shepard wrote: "chainsmoking, bald-pated long hair, with a full-flowing beard, sparkling eyes, and a gruff no-nonsense voice, given to wearing jump suits, Cossack shirts, and beaded necklaces, he looked like a combination of Santa Claus, Rasputin, elf, primordial Father Earth, sage, guru, perhaps Jehovah himself. By his own description a 'gypsy' and a seeker of new experiences, he had been through the drug scene, the Zen scene, and was still going strong within the sex scene."[7]

4. F. Perls, *Gestalt Therapy Verbatim* (Lafayette, CA: Real People Press, 1969), p. 4.
5. Abraham Maslow once said, "That man is crazy," after Perls started crawling on the floor during a talk Maslow was giving. [M. Shepard, *Fritz: An Intimate Portrait of Fritz Perls and Gestalt Therapy* (New York: Dutton, 1975), p. 158.]
6. Ibid., p. 220.
7. Ibid., p. 2.

Perls' life style and appearance may help explain his appeal, for they were in keeping with the mood of the late 1960s and early 1970s. But his phenomenal popularity was not based solely on the way he looked and acted. Rather, it was his admonition to live "here and now," to be oneself, that struck a responsive chord in a great many persons who were struggling to find a new center to their lives at a time when old centers and values had disintegrated.

When Perls was admitted to a hospital in Chicago in 1970, a police guard was required to keep away the horde of faithful followers milling anxiously around the building. They waited there for six days until he died. Whatever else is said about Perls, there is no denying the devotion of his followers, the adherence to the man and his principles that may be even stronger today than in 1970.

PERLS' APPROACH TO PERSONALITY: GESTALT THERAPY

Perls' approach to personality is a form of therapy rather than a theory about the nature of personality. However, as with Frankl, any form of therapy is based on some theory of how the personality functions.[8]

The best place to begin is with the word "Gestalt." This tells us much about what the system encompasses. "Gestalt" is a German word that can be translated as form, shape, or organization. It implies a sense of wholeness or completeness. The word became widely known when it was used to describe the school of thought in academic psychology that arose in Germany in the early years of the twentieth century. Gestalt psychology is concerned, in general, with the way in which we perceive the world around us. Our perception, Gestalt psychologists believe, is in terms of organized wholes or patterns.[9]

Perls' Gestalt Therapy did not derive directly from Gestalt psychology. Other than the use of the word "Gestalt," there is little in common between the two positions. Perls said that he admired some of the work of the earlier Gestalt psychologists, but he had read none of their books and only a few of their papers. He said he was not a "pure Gestaltist" and was never accepted by the academic Gestaltists.

There remains the word "Gestalt." Perls used it to denote the only law of human functioning which is constant and universal: every organism tends toward wholeness or completion. Anything which

8. The reader interested in Perls' therapeutic techniques should consult F. Perls, *Gestalt Therapy Verbatim* (Lafayette, CA: Real People Press, 1969).
9. A founder of Gestalt psychology, Max Wertheimer, was one of the two persons whose qualities inspired Maslow to study self-actualization (see Chapter 5, p. 59).

prevents or disrupts this Gestalt (or coming to closure) is harmful to the organism and leads to what Perls called an *unfinished situation,* which, of course, needs to be finished (made whole or complete).

All aspects of a person form a Gestalt and if they are kept from closure, the wholeness of the personality is shattered and the separate aspects may lose their meaning. A balance within the organism must be maintained in the interest of psychological health. Upset that balance—prevent the formation of a Gestalt—and some form of maladjustment will occur. And when we experience an imbalance we are motivated to correct it.

Thus, Perls proposed an entirely different motivational theory from that espoused by Freud. Freud believed that we are driven by a variety of instincts. Perls argued that we are driven by unfinished situations or incomplete Gestalts (such as his own lingering desire for a new confrontation with Freud). Each of us has a great many unfinished situations within us—perhaps hundreds—and it might seem that we should be hopelessly confused. With so many unfinished situations driving us, what keeps us from charging off in many directions at once?

We attend to these incomplete Gestalts in an orderly manner because we arrange them in a *hierarchy of importance.* The most urgent situation becomes the dominant controller and director of our thoughts and behavior until it is satisfied. Then the next most important one emerges, and so on.

Perls offered the example of a fire that broke out during one of his lectures. The fire immediately became more urgent than what he was talking about at the moment. The fire became the dominant unfinished situation, or the most important drive (to use traditional terminology). Now, if you run quickly from a fire you may find yourself out of breath. This means that a new unfinished situation takes precedence; your oxygen supply becomes more urgent than the danger of the fire. You slow down and take a breath for that need has become the director or controller of the moment.

One important aspect of dealing with unfinished situations is *self-regulation* versus *external regulation.* Healthy persons are able to do their own regulating, without interference from external forces, be it the needs or demands of others or the strictures of a social code. Self-awareness alone, Perls believed, can lead to the development and growth of a healthy personality. With full awareness of self, we are able to let our organism (the mind and body) take over and regulate our behavior. In a sense, we can come to rely on the wisdom of our own organism.

This requires that we recognize and accept our own impulses and yearnings. Perls believed that far too many people have been taught by their parents and their culture to inhibit their impulses and, as a result, they are afraid to express them. Yet inhibited impulses don't simply disappear; they manifest themselves in other ways. Thwarted aggressiveness, for example, may appear as a nervous tic, competitiveness as an ulcer, sexual longings as righteous propriety, and the need for independence as one or more phobias.

Instead of expressing our impulses spontaneously and naturally (thus completing the Gestalts), we *project* them onto other persons. We accuse others of doing or being what we would like to do or be. Timid persons accuse others of being aggressive, puritanical persons condemn the immorality of the young, bullies attack young men with long hair and accuse them of being homosexual. In each case, the person's unacceptable impulses are projected onto someone else.

Perls argued that in the interest of psychological health we must realize that these projections represent our inner feelings. We must be able to express our desires freely, with no external regulation or interference. We must learn what Perls calls "I am you." In other words, "I possess the needs for which I condemn you." More importantly, we must live in accordance with this principle.

Another aspect of Perls' approach to personality is the focus on the present as the only reality. Nothing exists for us, he believed, except the here and now. The past no longer exists and the future does not yet exist. Our memories of the past and anticipations of the future are experienced only in the present moment. Those who live as though the past were still with them, or who live as though the future were today, have unbalanced personalities. They are living in a time that is no longer real or not yet real, sacrificing the present for a time that does not exist.

When we do not have an adequate understanding of ourselves in the here and now, we are driven to escape to the past or the future. Both moves are harmful to full human development.

If we live in the past (the *retrospective character*) we may become overly sentimental about some period in our lives or blame our parents for everything. This is a tragic mistake, according to Perls, and the most frequent unfinished situation we carry with us. We may blame our parents all our lives, holding them responsible for our problems. In this case we still think of ourselves as children, not as adults responsible for, and to, ourselves. In order to complete the Gestalt we must let go of our parents and say, in effect, "I am an adult now. I am responsible for my own life." We must recognize that our memories are not reality.

Equally harmful to full human growth is living in the future, the *prospective character*. Fantasies about what lies ahead are no more real than memories of the past. We cannot experience the future any more than we can re-experience the past. We can only have images of these time periods. If our visions and hopes for the future are not fulfilled we are disappointed and unhappy and may blame other persons or circumstances or "bad luck" for our fate. Again we are shifting responsibility for our lives to someone or something other than ourselves.

If our view is backward or forward, we are sacrificing the present moment and the enjoyment and satisfactions it could bring. The here and now is the only reality we have and we must take the responsibility for immersing ourselves fully in each moment and benefiting from its experiences.

While Perls argues that we must live fully in the present, he is not advocating that we totally abandon our memories or our visions of the future. The past contains unfinished situations which we must finish, joyful experiences which are pleasurable to recall, and experiences which can help us adapt to the present. We must be aware of the past but we must not live there.

So it is with the future. We must plan for the future—we could not grow otherwise—but we must not use that planning as a substitute for the present.

This, then, is the essence of Perls' approach to personality. We are motivated to regulate our internal balances; in other words, to finish unfinished situations. In order to do that, we must accept our impulses and yearnings and deal with them (as with all aspects of life) in the here and now, the present. Note that the focus is very much on self. We alone have the responsibility for directing our lives. We must not abdicate that responsibility.

ADDITIONAL ASPECTS OF THE PERSONALITY

Perls believed that we function on two levels: the *public* level (overt behavior) and the *private* level (thought and fantasy). Thinking is a means of rehearsing for future behavior, trying out things in the private level of our mind. While necessary in order to plan for the future, such silent rehearsing can lead to *anxiety*, the tension that exists between "now" and "then." Few of us can tolerate this tension so we try to anticipate the future in such a way as to make it an extension of today. In other words, we try to hold onto the familiar, to preserve the status quo, which, in turn, prevents further human growth.

The healthy personality lives in and of the moment and, although capable of planning for the future, is not bothered by anxiety over what may happen tomorrow.

Guilt also plays a role in Perls' theory. He defines it as resentment projected onto others. Resentment is an important notion in determining psychological health because it is a common unexpressed experience. Anything which needs to be expressed and is not makes us uncomfortable. Resentments are one of the worst kinds of unfinished situation we carry with us. Persons who are resentful have reached an impasse; they are "stuck," as Perls put it. They cannot move forward and deal with the target of the resentment nor can they forget what is upsetting them. The obvious solution is to express the resentment; that is the only way to move beyond the impasse and be relieved of the guilt which the resentment causes.

We have noted the importance of *awareness* for psychological health. We must be aware of our unfinished situations, of our impulses and yearnings, of the here and now, of our resentments. There are three levels of awareness: awareness of the *self,* awareness of the *world,* and awareness of the *intervening fantasy* between the self and the world. Perls called this intermediate level the DMZ (demilitarized zone) and it functions to keep us from being totally in touch with ourselves and our world.

The DMZ contains our prejudices, the prejudgments through which we view the world and other people. If you look at the world through your own biases, you don't see the world as it is but only as it appears to you.

Healthy persons are in total contact with their awareness of the self and awareness of the world. Disturbed persons, however, are out of touch with both of these levels of awareness. The DMZ, the intervening fantasy level of awareness, can consume so much energy with its fantasies that there is little left for the reality of the self and of the world. Psychological health can be achieved by understanding those aspects of our personality which are fantasy and irrational and then emptying out this intermediate zone, dropping the barrier between the world of reality and the self so that we can see things as they really are.

When this can be achieved, an amazing transformation takes place. "Suddenly the world is *there*. . . . The aim in therapy, the growth aim, is to lose more and more of your 'mind' and come more to your *senses*."[10] We come to experience our selves and our world of the moment, instead of our fantasies, fears, and prejudices.

10.   F. Perls, *Gestalt Therapy Verbatim* (Lafayette, CA: Real People Press, 1969), p. 50.

To accomplish this goal we must establish a *continuum of awareness* so that we may proceed with our most important task: finishing the unfinished situations in life. To establish this awareness continuum we have to be alert to what is going on around us. We must not lose our awareness of the here and now, even for a moment.

However, our awareness of the here and now can become unpleasant or threatening; we may see things we don't want to see. We may then try to interrupt our awareness of the present by replacing an unpleasant awareness through escaping into the past or the future, by intellectualizing, or by engaging our mind in a meaningless jumble of free associations and truly experiencing none of them. Perls calls these means of avoiding the present awareness *dissociation,* defined as an avoidance or flight from reality. Dissociation represents a *phobic attitude.* Most of us prefer to avoid unpleasant situations and so we utilize all sorts of armor and masks, but as soon as we do this, we interrupt our awareness continuum, withdrawing our attention from the here and now. This phobic attitude is an enemy of human development. Our focus must be drawn again to the present, no matter how painful it is.

Let us now return to the matter of self-regulation versus external regulation; we saw how self-regulation is vital for the development of a healthy personality. As children, we learn from our parents a set of rules, one way of behaving which brings us approval and another way which brings disapproval or even punishment. We usually call this set of rules our conscience. Freud called it the superego.

Perls was opposed to the idea of external control or regulation of behavior. We should not be told—by others or by ourselves—that we must behave one way or another. Even when we have internalized these rules we are still being led by external forces because they are originally external to us. Perls called these internalized external controls the *topdog,* because they dictate to us what we should be like and how we should behave.

The topdog is dictatorial and righteous; it always knows best. Perls called it a bully because it manipulates us with commands and threatens us with catastrophe if we violate its dictates. If you don't behave in accordance with the topdog, it retaliates; it says, "you won't be loved, you won't go to heaven, you will die."[11]

Perls criticized Freud for his emphasis on only the superego, or topdog, as a force in personality while neglecting the opposite force, the *underdog.* The underdog also manipulates us but in more subtle

11.   Ibid., p. 18.

and coaxing ways. The underdog becomes defensive and apologetic and says to the topdog, "I try my best. . . . I can't help it if I fail. . . . I have such good intentions."[12]

The topdog is the more powerful of these two "clowns," but the underdog is more cunning and, as a result, usually wins out over the topdog. There is in most of us a continuing battle between them for control of the personality and we become divided into the controller and the one being controlled. The conflict is never finished, Perls believed, and leads to the *self-torture game.*

In this internal game we believe that the topdog is always correct and we are led to follow its demands. We feel badly if we are unable to do so. Unfortunately, many of the topdog's commands are oriented toward perfection and thus are impossible to follow. In fact, Perls wrote that insanity, or at least severe neurosis, will result from trying to follow these perfectionist commands.

We must become aware of this split in our personality between the underdog and the topdog and reconcile their differences. Once we accomplish that, we will realize how impossible it is for us to deliberately change our nature to conform to standards propounded by others or by society. Too many people dedicate their lives to fulfilling or actualizing an image of what they think they should be like, of how their topdog tells them they should behave.

What we must try to actualize is our true inner selves. There is a profound difference between actualization of the self and actualization of an image of the self. Too many of us, Perls believed, live only for the image we carry because we have lost our true sense of self. The self has been overshadowed by our frantic effort to live up to an ideal. We must be what we really are. The topdog and the image of the self it fashions try to get us to be someone we are not. This is the "curse of the ideal."[13]

Every form of external control, even those which have been internalized, interferes with the development of psychological health for it thwarts the fulfillment of the self. The only thing which should guide us in our behavior is the situation we are in at any given moment. The only way we can cope with the complexities of life is to let the present situation control our actions.

Perls offered the illustration of driving a car. We do not drive the same way all the time; for example, at the same high speed. Instead, our speed is controlled by the situation. We drive faster on an

12. Ibid.
13. Ibid., p. 19.

open highway where there is little traffic and slower on a crowded city street or when we are tired. We respond to each situation. If we are truly in touch with the realities of self and the world then the situation, and our own natural and spontaneous response to it, is sufficient to guide us. But if we are controlled by external forces we respond to all situations in the same predetermined manner, behaving in accordance with our self-image rather than with our true self.

Another aspect of Perls' view of personality is the *ego boundary*, which is concerned with the relationship of the organism to the environment. A boundary separates one thing from another; it forms an exclusivity, keeping things apart. Similarly, the ego boundary differentiates or separates the self from the rest of the world.

Two characteristics of the ego boundary are *identification* and *alienation*. We identify with the ego (our self) and place a high value on that which pertains or belongs to the self. We identify with our house, family, car, or profession, and clearly distinguish these from the houses, families, cars, or professions of other persons. These identifications are usually strong, particularly those with the family. For example, if some member of our family has been insulted, we feel insulted ourselves. We can also identify with friends, club or church members, co-workers, and the like.

Within the ego boundary there are the feelings of love, solidarity, and cohesion. These positive feelings do not extend to those on the other side of the boundary. Persons who are not our friends, or who belong to a different political party, may be treated with unfriendliness, suspicion, even hostility and rejection. "Get out of my house," we may say. "Go back where you came from. We don't want your kind in our neighborhood."

The ego boundary thus sets up a polarity of attraction and repulsion. What is inside the boundary is familiar and good; what is outside is strange and bad. ("Your god is false, my God is real.") We identify with what is inside our ego boundary and are alienated from all the rest.

The ego boundary applies to all areas of life and in healthier persons it is always capable of being changed. If, for example, you work with members of a minority group and lose your prejudice against them, then the ego boundary which had previously excluded them comes to include them, thus creating a new boundary. Persons who cling to their prejudices and are closed to new experiences retain their ego boundaries.

The ego boundary also applies within the self. We may exclude parts of our selves from the area within our ego boundary. For example, we may be unable to accept that some of our thoughts, feelings, or desires truly belong to us. We reject or disown them. "That's not me. I don't have such desires." We may project these unacceptable impulses onto other people.

The way in which we reject these troublesome impulses is less important than the fact that we are disowning part of our nature, a portion of our selves. Our internal ego boundary has become smaller. We identify with only a portion of our nature and are alienated from the rest. As a result, we are no longer truly ourselves. We are using only a portion of our qualities or characteristics.

Perls believed that this constriction of the internal ego boundary explains why most of us use such a small portion of our human potential. We are not totally and fully ourselves. As our ego boundary shrinks, our energy or power (our "life force") decreases. Consequently, we function at a reduced capacity, not unlike an eight-cylinder car trying to run on only four cylinders; it may still move, but not very well or fast.

Supremely healthy individuals have rejected or discarded none of their potential; it is all available for use. Such persons are in touch with all aspects of their selves and find none of them offending or threatening. Healthy persons are fully themselves, fully aware, and fully in use.

When we are fully experiencing our selves, external ego boundaries seem to disintegrate. We are, at that moment, totally absorbed in existing. There is an integration of the subjective and the objective, the self and the world, a fusion into expanded awareness, heightened sensitivity, and full immersion in the processes of the moment, the here and now.

THE DEVELOPMENT OF PERSONALITY

The basic principle of Perls' view of the development of personality is the change to self-support from environmental support. Before birth we are totally dependent on the environment of the womb for support. The fetus supplies nothing to itself. This changes at the instant of birth when the infant is forced to breathe on its own. For a brief period at birth we experience the first symptom of the *impasse*, an important Gestalt Therapy concept. The impasse represents the crucial point where environmental support is no longer available and self-support is not yet available; the infant must die or learn to breathe on its own.

As the infant grows, it continues to demand environmental

support. Gradually, however, the need for environmental support diminishes as the child learns to do more for itself. It learns to crawl, speak, and walk, and develops more of its own inner resources, its potential. The child becomes less dependent on others and its support comes increasingly from the self. Freeing ourselves from environmental support in a physical sense occurs naturally and is not difficult. Freeing ourselves from environmental support in a psychological and social sense, however, presents great problems and leads to the "basic conflict" of human existence.

This conflict is between what we are and what others want us to be. Perls believed that all living organisms—plants, animals, humans—have one innate goal: to actualize the self as it really is, in accordance with its own nature. Perls noted that a rose fulfills itself as a rose and not as a kangaroo, and an elephant fulfills itself as an elephant and not as a bird. As human beings we actualize ourselves by fully living our unique potential, by being what we are and not something else.

The conflict arises because we live in a society which may expect us to be something other than what we are. Society, in the form of its representatives (parents, teachers, and the like), may prevent the natural, spontaneous, and full actualization of the self, what Perls calls "authentic growth." They may "falsify" our existence through the use of two powerful tools, the *stick* and *hypnosis*.

The stick works through the principle of *catastrophic expectation*, pointing out the disasters which will befall us if we behave as we wish rather than as society wishes. We are reminded that if we do as we please ("I'll tell them what I really think of them"), the consequences are unpleasant ("They won't love me anymore").

Hypnosis involves an attempt at propaganda or persuasion such as is found in the classroom, the pulpit, or advertisements, an appeal for you to believe something. Perls described the process vividly in one of his lectures: "Right now . . . I am hypnotizing you into believing what I say. I don't give you the chance to digest, to assimilate, to taste what I say. You hear from my voice that I try to cast a spell on you, to slip my 'wisdom' into your guts until you either assimilate it or puke, or feed it into your computer and say: "That's an interesting concept.' "[14]

Whether through the stick or hypnosis, we are dependent on the environment rather than our selves for support, and full expression of our potential is inhibited.

As children grow they face one of two situations: being spoiled

14.   Ibid., p. 32.

or overcoming frustration. Children can easily be spoiled. Parents may answer all the child's questions rather than let it seek answers on its own. Or they can give the child everything it desires and thus fail to frustrate the child. Perls thought frustration is desirable for the growing child. Without frustration there is no reason for the child to develop abilities and discover the thrill of being able to do something on its own.

Perls believed that children are "stuck" when they are spoiled or do not experience sufficient frustration. Instead of using their unique potential to grow and develop, these children use it to control the environment, especially the parents. They use their energy to manipulate their parents for support. Again, they are dependent on the environment rather than on the self.

When children learn effective means of manipulation, they have acquired *character*. And the more fixed a character we have, the less unique potential we can express because our behavior has become rigid and predictable.

There are several characters that children may develop. They may demand "directional support" from others, saying, in effect, "I don't know what to do. Mommy or Daddy, what shall I do?" They may cry or throw temper tantrums to manipulate the parents or appeal to the parents' self-esteem, to flatter them so they will give something in return. Another character is to play helpless, saying, in effect, "I'm certain you can help me. You are so wise." These behaviors carry into adulthood where the person plays the same games of dependency.

When we constantly need praise, affection, or encouragement from others, they become our masters. We are neither dependent upon or in control of ourselves. We are constantly concerned with impressing someone else. Their opinion of us becomes more important than what we think of ourselves.

We are no longer able to behave spontaneously and naturally. We have to wear a mask, play a role. We have to plan and rehearse everything we say and do, sensitive to the effect it will have on someone else. These roles, through constant repetition, become habits. To manipulate the environment through playing roles in order to get support is a sign of neurosis and immaturity. The energy that has to be invested in this manipulation is no longer available for our own development. We become slaves, looking to receive from others what we cannot give ourselves.

The healthy alternative is to substitute self-support for environmental support. This task is the ultimate goal of personality development. We must cease playing roles for others and actualize our potential by behaving in ways that truly reflect our inner nature. When we have done that we have reached Perls' version of supreme psychological health. Perls did not give this state a name so I will call it the "here and now" person.

THE NATURE OF THE "HERE AND NOW" PERSON

Perls did not offer a list of characteristics of the psychologically healthy person, but they can easily be inferred from his views on personality. The here and now person is *securely grounded in the present moment of existence*. Recognizing that the only reality we have is of the moment, such persons have no need to look backward or forward to find meaning or purpose in life. They are not prisoners of events in the past or of fantasies and visions of the future. Their focus, awareness, and satisfaction depend on their second-by-second existence in the real world.

Psychologically healthy persons have a *full awareness and acceptance of who and what they are*. They understand and accept their strengths and weaknesses and are aware of their potentials as human beings. They know what they have the ability to do and to be. Equally important, they know what they cannot do or be and they do not try to be something they are not. They do not maintain ideals or goals they know they cannot reach.

Not only do they recognize and accept themselves, but they are also able to *express their impulses and yearnings* openly and fully without inhibition or guilt. Less healthy persons cannot express certain aspects of their being and instead project them onto others. Psychologically healthy persons are sufficiently secure to let everyone know what they are feeling or thinking or desiring at any moment.

Healthy persons are capable of *taking responsibility for their own lives*. In that sense, they are "on their own" and do not shift the responsibility for who and what they are to their parents, spouses, fate, or any external source. They recognize that they alone are responsible for what they make of their lives, for everything they say, do, feel, or think.

Allied with this, healthy persons *shed responsibility for anyone else*. Just as no one else is responsible for your life, so are you not responsible for anyone else. As Perls noted in the Gestalt prayer, "I do my thing and you do your thing." He argued that if we take responsibility for another person we become omnipotent and interfering in their

life. We will tend to support them and this diminishes their independence and their sense of responsibility for themselves. We should
interact with others naturally and honestly by being what we are and
letting them be what they are. "You are you and I am I."

Healthy persons are completely *in touch with the self and the world*.
They are in touch with their senses and feelings and with what is going on around them. Their awareness is not clouded by fantasies that
constitute the DMZ. The unhealthy person is out of touch with both
of those realities, particularly with the self, and the energies are
consumed by fantasies of the intermediate zone of awareness.
Healthy persons dwell less in this intermediate mental world and
more in the real world as it is relayed to them through the sense
organs. Perls urged that we must lose our minds and come to our
senses; in other words, be in touch with reality.

Here and now persons are able to *express their resentments* openly.
In less healthy persons, resentments are the most common unexpressed experiences.[15]

While psychologically healthy persons are fully in touch with the
world around them, they are *free of external regulation* of their lives.
They are not guided by or dictated to by anyone else's conception of
proper behavior. Less healthy persons continue to be commanded by
the values of their parents in the form of the conscience. Here and
now persons are not trying to fulfill an image of the self but rather
express and fulfill the true self. They have given up environmental
support for self support and do not rely on external standards or
values. Their behavior is spontaneous and natural, reflecting who and
what they are, not what someone else thinks they should be.

Here and now persons are *guided by and react to the situation of the
moment.* Such persons respond flexibly and realistically because they
are fully in touch with reality. They sense all aspects of a situation objectively because they do not see it through irrational fantasies or the
prescriptions of others.

Psychologically healthy persons are characterized by an *absence of
constricted ego boundaries.* Their ego boundaries are flexible, capable of
extension or enlargement. This openness applies to external ego
boundaries (the environment) and internal ego boundaries (the self).
No thoughts or feelings are excluded by the ego boundary. No aspect
of the self is denied or disowned. Healthy persons accept all aspects of

15. Perls was a living example of his view of psychological health and certainly capable
of expressing his resentments. He was often curt and rude; if someone bored him
he would say, "I never asked to be introduced to you," and walk away. [M.
Shepard, *Fritz* (New York: Dutton, 1975), p. 9.]

their nature and thus can use all their potential for further growth and development.

Here and now persons are *not engaged in the pursuit of happiness.* Perls argued that it is wrong to pursue happiness for it cannot be achieved. To make happiness a goal is to divert energy and attention from our only reality, the present. While it is not a goal of psychologically healthy persons, happiness does occur although it is transitory and sporadic. Perls insisted that happiness simply happens and it is impossible, and perhaps undesirable, for it to become a permanent condition. The pursuit of happiness for its own sake is doomed and leads only the ersatz happiness of "prefabricated fun *à la* Disneyland." We shouldn't *pursue* happiness; we should just *be* who and what we are at the moment.

A Personal Comment

Of all the theorists discussed in this book, Fritz Perls has one of the largest and most enthusiastic public followings. While other theorists—Allport, Maslow, Rogers, Jung—have been better received by academic psychology, none has had the popular impact of Perls. Although Perls is rarely given recognition within academic psychology, his work has been extremely influential in the human potential/human growth movement in the United States.

Gestalt training centers have sprung up all over the country and scores, perhaps hundreds, of seminars are given each year. Thousands of persons have participated in Gestalt Therapy and the number is clearly growing. Perls' approach (and the man himself) seems to represent the current values and unmet needs of many of us.

This leads to an interesting question about the future of Gestalt Therapy, now that it is without its leader. Perls was such an unusually skillful individual, so forceful and dynamic, sensitive and intuitive in his clinical interactions, that his death has left a void in the Gestalt movement. One Gestalt therapist wrote, "In the wake of Perls's death, the Gestalt Movement . . . looks a bit like an anthill that has been uncovered. People are scurrying about uncertain how to proceed. There is no clear leadership."[16]

A similar situation occurred in psychoanalysis following the death of Freud. Both Freud and Perls were strong-willed men whose

16. W. Kempler, "Gestalt Theory," in R. Corsini, ed., *Current Psychotherapies* (Itasca, Ill.: F. E. Peacock, 1973), p. 253.

leadership was not effectively challenged during their lifetime. Their death, in a sense, left their ships with neither captain nor rudder. In psychoanalysis there was much confusion when the master died. Eventually, after several decades, younger psychoanalysts produced noticeable changes in Freud's position while nevertheless retaining the core of his teachings. It was a slow but necessary process to separate the movement from the man. Presumably, a similar separation is occurring now in Gestalt Therapy and I look forward to learning what changes will be introduced as various individuals and groups promote their own views.

In any event, there is strong interest in the Perls stage of the Gestalt Therapy movement. It speaks of human potential and ways of achieving it, and of a style of behaving and feeling—with respect to oneself and to the rest of the world—that seems to be in step with our time and place. Doing one's "own thing" is a prescription for health that many have taken seriously, and perhaps it has led to a generation of people more candid with themselves and with others, more spontaneous, and possessing a greater sense of personal freedom than that enjoyed by past generations. (Whether this is to their ultimate benefit is an open question.)

Let us examine some of the major points of the Gestalt position. First, recognizing and accepting our impulses and yearnings, weaknesses and strengths, is an idea proposed by other personality theorists. It does seem healthier to have an objective picture of ourselves, to see ourselves as we are and not as we wish to be. Here and now persons live realistically in this regard, with a clear, objective picture of their nature.

I am troubled, however, by Perls' advice that it is not enough to be aware of our impulses, that we must also express them openly. We must not thwart or inhibit our impulses but must act as we are impelled to, apparently in disregard of the possible effects on others. If your urge is to do your own thing, and you believe that it is honest and natural for you to do so, then what extreme behaviors might you not excuse as your right? After all, you're just being yourself. Perls acted this way himself and no doubt hurt others in the process.

We cannot be careful every moment of our lives lest we say or do something to offend someone else, but neither should we be deliberately thoughtless toward others whenever we feel like it. Not only might we unnecessarily harm someone else, but the retaliation might be harmful to us. It seems to me that to be able to follow this prescription fully—to express every impulse when it appears—requires a great deal of freedom from retaliation, an independence from the rest of the world. You would have to be in a position where no one else can hurt you—fire you from your job, lower your grade, overcharge you for repairs (the many personal interactions where what you get or how you are treated may depend on how pleasant you are). I can applaud this idea of expressing our impulses but am concerned about the practicalities of doing so on a daily basis. Life is not a Gestalt workshop or sensitivity session; the people around you in the real world may not be as forgiving of your behavior.

What about living in the here and now? Perls wrote, "there is no other reality than the present," and this seems a concise statement of fact. What else do we have to experience—to hear, taste, smell, see, and feel—but the present moment of existence? If we don't make full use of it we will never have another chance; it will not return. Awareness of the experiences of the moment seems a primary requisite for psychological health. How much more productive it is than lamenting the past or dwelling in the imaginary world of the future. Yet, as Perls noted, we must not forget yesterday or ignore tomorrow; either course would be unrealistic. To remember the past or plan for the future is not to live there.

It is easy to agree with Perls' contention that psychologically healthy persons are completely in touch with the realities of self and the external world. It is inherent in his view that the here and now person perceives these realities objectively, mirroring them as they are, not subjectively distorting them. Apparently it is because of this objective perception that psychologically healthy persons can be guided by the situation of the moment and their spontaneous reaction to it.

As a consequence of knowing themselves, such persons are able to actualize their true selves rather than an ideal or image of what they should be. It clearly seems healthier to be ourselves than to be what others expect us to be. It seems more satisfying to be self-regulated than to be regulated by others.

What about Perls' notion of responsibility? Part of his view seems to me to be desirable but another part seems abhorrent. It is difficult to argue with the view that we should be responsible for the course and conduct of our own lives. Surely we cannot abdicate to an outside force, nor is it healthy to blame others (usually parents) for the way we are. I think Perls' point is good; no one else is responsible for what we are and how we behave. It has become fashionable, since Freud, to blame unhappiness or failure on a bad childhood (a rejecting mother, no father, sibling rivalry, too harsh toilet training, too lenient toilet training, no bicycle, and so on). It is easy and ultimately self-defeating to shift the blame to someone or something else.

Perls' notion of individual responsibility for our lives is a refreshing antidote to positions which depict human beings as passive victims of past circumstances. Healthier societies might be the result if everyone believed that what he or she is today (and will be twenty years from now) is strictly a matter of personal responsibility.

However, I seriously doubt that better societies or individuals would result from Perls' related view that we must shed responsibility for anyone else. This strikes me as a totally selfish, uncaring position in which persons live solely for themselves, with no obligation toward fellow human beings. Many writers have offered similar criticisms, including some Gestalt therapists (among them, Perls' wife). William Schutz, the well-known Esalen psychologist and one-time associate of Perls, commented on the Gestalt prayer and the notion of abdicating responsibility for others: "I'm disappointed that it's so influential. I think it's had a negative effect as well as positive—a kind of 'Fuck you' attitude."[17] This is one aspect of Perls' position that I hope will be tempered as Gestalt Therapy develops. Responsibility for one's self is certainly vital, but as long as we live among others, influencing and depending on them, responsibility for others seems equally vital.

My final criticism of Perls' approach is that it seems anti-intellectual. Reason and logic do not loom large in his prescription for psychological health. The emphasis is on feeling and being, existing not thinking. "Lose your mind and come to your senses." He wrote that the intellect has become "the whore of intelligence . . . the poor, pallid substitute for the vivid immediacy of sensing and experiencing."[18]

We should rely more on the wisdom of the organism (which is intuitive and based on emotion and feeling) than on rational thinking. The intellect, Perls felt, is too concerned with answering the question of why things happen, thus limiting our ability to fully experience how things happen. Explaining things intellectually, he argued, is of less value than understanding them intuitively. However, many would seriously question this reduced emphasis on the powers of logic and reason.

Despite these criticisms, I am intrigued with much of Perls' work. There is both an intellectual and an intuitive appeal in many of his prescriptions for a healthy personality. It seems hard to deny that living in full awareness of the present, being objectively in touch with ourselves and the world around us, accepting who and what we are, taking responsibility for our own lives, and being guided by ourselves rather than by external forces, are characteristics of a healthy person.

I am also impressed by the warning Perls issued against some

17. M. Shepard, *Fritz* (New York: Dutton, 1975), p. 4. Schutz is the author of *Joy: Expanding Human Awareness* (New York: Grove Press, 1967).
18. F. Perls, "Workshop vs. Individual Therapy," *Journal of Long Island Consultation Center*, 1967, *15* (2), p. 15.

aspects of the human potential movement. He became concerned, toward the end of his life, about quacks and charlatans practicing Gestalt Therapy, using gimmicks rather than substance, promising instant "turn ons" and overnight cures. He was alarmed that his approach to therapy was becoming faddish and might do more harm than good if practiced by persons not thoroughly versed in the Gestalt point of view. He was disturbed lest people take Gestalt Therapy to be an instant cure, a promise of immediate sensory awareness, or a license to pursue a totally hedonistic state, with fun, pleasure, and ecstasy as the only goals of life. Perls argued that the goals of his Gestalt Therapy are more serious: to promote the full growth and development of human potential. And that cannot be accomplished rapidly through drugs or shortcuts. The process of becoming fully human takes time, effort, and discipline.

I repeat, I am impressed by a great deal of Perls' writings. It is unfortunate, however, that the Gestalt prayer has assumed such prominence. It may be a gross oversimplification of Perls' program for human potential and may even be misleading for it tends to overshadow his serious philosophy of what we are and what we can become.

To counteract the Gestalt prayer I offer some lines from Perls' autobiography, *In and Out of the Garbage Pail.* To me, they represent far more constructive advice.

Friend, don't be a perfectionist. Perfectionism is a curse and a strain. For you tremble lest you miss the bull's-eye. You are perfect if you let be.

Friend, don't be afraid of mistakes. Mistakes are not sins. Mistakes are ways of doing something different, perhaps creatively new.

Friend, don't be sorry for your mistakes. Be proud of them. You had the courage to give something of yourself. . . .

Beware of both extremes, perfectionism as well as instant cure, instant joy, instant sensory awareness. . . .

Beware of any helpers. Helpers are con-men who promise something for nothing. They spoil you and keep you dependent and immature.

BIBLIOGRAPHY

Perls, F. *Ego, Hunger, and Aggression: The Beginning of Gestalt Therapy.* New York: Random House, 1947.

——. *Gestalt Therapy Verbatim.* Lafayette, CA: Real People Press, 1969.

——. *In and Out of the Garbage Pail.* Lafayette, CA: Real People Press, 1969; New York: Bantam, 1972.

——. *The Gestalt Approach; Eyewitness to Therapy.* Ben Lomond, CA: Science and Behavior Books, 1973.

Shepard, M. *Fritz: An Intimate Portrait of Fritz Perls and Gestalt Therapy.* New York: Dutton, 1975.

9

The nature of
psychological health

In Chapter One I asked the question "What is the healthy personality?" Now it is time to take up the question again, for it has not been answered definitively. And for good reason; there is no single prescription for or description of psychological health on which all psychologists or personality theorists would agree.

We have discussed seven visions of the healthy personality and there are points of difference as well as agreement among them. Some theorists argue that our perception of ourselves and the world around us must be objective; others urge that healthy persons take their own subjective view of reality as the basis for behavior. Some argue that we can't be psychologically healthy without an intense involvement in some form of work; others make no mention of the worth of work. And there is even disagreement on what many might consider a basic component of being fully human: the matter of responsibility for others. Two theorists don't discuss this point and a third argues for the deliberate abandonment of responsibility for others. In addition, the theorists differ on the major motivating force in human life.

Finding differences among these theorists is easy; finding points of similarity takes some effort. Perhaps the only point on which they agree fully is that psychologically healthy persons are in conscious control of their lives. Healthy persons are capable of consciously, if not always rationally, directing their behavior and being in charge of their own destinies. We are not motivated chiefly by unconscious forces of which we are unaware and unable to control. Even Jung, who alone among these theorists stressed the importance of the unconscious, noted that these invisible forces must be brought into conscious awareness, although they should not dominate consciousness.

In one form or another, these theorists also seem to agree that psychologically healthy persons know who and what they are. Such persons are aware of their strengths and weaknesses, virtues and vices, and, in general, are tolerant and accepting of them. They do not pretend to be something they are not. While they may play social roles to meet the requirements of other people or situations (except in Perls' view), they do not confuse these roles with their true selves.

Another generally agreed upon characteristic of psychological health is a firm anchoring in the present. While most of the theorists believe that we are not immune to influences of the past (particularly childhood), none argues that we are immutably shaped by early experiences. Psychologically healthy persons do not live in the past. They are not continuing victims of real or imagined rejections or conflicts that may have occurred before the age of five.

Several theorists emphasize a view toward the future as vital to a healthy personality. But they do not urge us to substitute the future for the present. Our orientation should be toward future goals and missions, but we must be aware of and alive to our ongoing existence.

A less clear but still prominent emphasis is on the importance of increasing rather than reducing tension through contact with increasingly diverse forms of sensory and imaginal stimulation. Psychologically healthy persons do not long for quiet and stability but for challenge and excitement in life, for new goals and new experiences.

As noted earlier, these similarities are not unanimous; some theorists have not made themselves clear on all these points. In order to make these viewpoints easier to compare, I have prepared the table on the opposite page.

This still does not answer the question "What is the healthy personality?" But perhaps the question is misleading. Perhaps there is no such thing as *the* healthy personality, no universal prescription for psychological health that works in the same way for everyone. We are not carbon copies or duplicate prints of one another in our neuroses or in our more normal behavior. Why should we be thought to be alike in our forms of psychological health? If there is one constant about human nature on which most psychologists would agree it is its idiosyncratic nature; each of us is unique.

Thus, there may not be a single version or approach to psychological health that fits everyone, just as a single drug will not have the same effect even though all those taking it may have the same disease. The drug will work for some people and their health will be improved; it will produce no effect on others and be harmful to still others.

Models of the Healthy Personality—A Comparison of Characteristics*

Characteristic	Allport	Rogers	Fromm	Maslow	Jung	Frankl	Perls
Motivation	Intentions toward future	Self-actualization	Productivity	Self-actualization	Self-realization	Meaning	To be here and now
Conscious or unconscious focus	Conscious	Conscious	Conscious	Conscious	Both	Conscious	Conscious
Emphasis on past	No	No	Yes	No	Yes	No	No
Emphasis on present	Yes	Yes	Yes	Yes	Yes	Yes	Yes
Emphasis on future	Yes	No	(?)	(?)	Yes	Yes	No
Emphasis on increasing or reducing tension	Increasing	Increasing	(?)	Increasing	(?)	Increasing	(?)
Role of work and goals	Vital	None	(?)	Vital	(?)	Vital	None
Nature of perception	Objective	Subjective	Objective	Objective	Objective	(?)	Objective
Responsibility for others	Yes	(?)	Yes	Yes	(?)	Yes	No

*(?) indicates that the theorist has not made himself clear on this point, or that I did not find any discussion of that issue in his writings.

A similar case can be made for sensitivity sessions, T-groups, and the like, which are touted as new, miraculous ways to psychological health. Some persons do indeed find a richer, more fulfilling life through these growth encounters. Others leave with no sudden self-insight or outburst of self-actualization. Some end such sessions in worse shape than when they began. Surely the same can be said for these seven prescriptions for psychological health.

The effects of these approaches to a healthy personality differ not only for different persons, but also for the same person at different ages. Our values, wants, needs, fears, and hopes change enormously as we progress from one stage of development to the next. From childhood to adolescence to young adulthood to middle age to old age, our personalities continue to grow. What we want for ourselves at twenty may be inappropriate at forty. Just as I am not a duplicate of you, so I am not a duplicate of the self I was twenty years ago.

This means, of course, that the presciption for psychological health that works best at one age may be a dismal failure at a later point in life. It may, for example, be healthy at age twenty to be a Perls' here and now person, concerned with the pleasures and experiences of the moment, with little thought for tomorrow or for others. At age forty, however, we may find fulfillment only by confronting the unconscious or finding a meaning to life.

Ideally, we never stop growing. (This may be another characteristic of psychological health—neurotics have stagnant personalities.) We undergo new experiences and we change as a result, if we are truly open to the world. The clothing, activities, and values of the seventeen-year-old no longer fit the thirty-five-year-old. Why, then, should we expect the teenager's route to a healthy personality to be the path for the mature adult?

But how do we find the right path at each stage of growth? I suspect that we find it in the same way we learn what is appropriate for us in every sphere of life. We try out different life styles, sets of beliefs, and social roles, to see how they fit. The persons who seem to have the greatest chance of achieving psychological health are those who are free enough (secure enough with their selves) to experiment with different prescriptions to see which ones are validated in the laboratory of their daily lives. Others can suggest a course to follow, but only you can tell how well it works.

index